歐盟CBAM法規：
台灣廠商因應之道與申報準備

陳麗娟 著

歐盟CBAM法規：
台灣廠商因應之道與申報準備

國家圖書館出版品預行編目（CIP）資料

歐盟CBAM法規：台灣廠商因應之道與申報準備/
陳麗娟 著. -- 初版. -- 高雄市：麗文文化事業股份
有限公司, 2023.07
　　面；　公分
ISBN 978-986-490-218-7（平裝）

1.CST: 歐洲聯盟　2.CST: 貿易法規　3.CST: 碳排放

558.2　　　　　　　　　　　　　112009164

作　　　者　陳麗娟

發 行 人　楊宏文
編　　輯　沈志翰
封 面 設 計　毛湘萍
內 文 排 版　菩薩蠻數位文化有限公司

出 版 者　麗文文化事業股份有限公司
　　　　　802019 高雄市苓雅區五福一路 57 號 2 樓之 2
　　　　　電話：07-2265267
　　　　　傳真：07-2233073
　　　　　購書專線：07-2265267 轉 236
　　　　　E-mail：order@liwen.com.tw
　　　　　LINE ID：@sxs1780d
　　　　　線上購書：https://www.chuliu.com.tw/

臺北分公司　100003 臺北市中正區重慶南路一段 57 號 10 樓之 12
　　　　　電話：02-29222396
　　　　　傳真：02-29220464

法 律 顧 問　林廷隆律師
　　　　　電話：02-29658212

刷　　次　初版一刷‧2023年7月
定　　價　600元
I S B N　978-986-490-218-7（平裝）

目錄 CONTENTS

第三章

主管機關

第四章

CBAM憑證

PART 3 CBAM英文條文

CHAPTER XI

FINAL PROVISIONS

PART 1

前言

歐盟為國際社會對抗氣候變遷的先驅，2019年12月公布的歐洲綠色政綱（European Green Deal）擬定了明確的路徑，實現在2030年降低至1990年水準55%的碳排放目標，在2050年以前成為氣候中和的大陸。氣候變遷是全球的問題需要有全球的解決方案，碳洩漏（carbon leakage）產生的原因，是高碳排企業將生產外移到氣候政策寬鬆的國家；或進口高碳排的產品取代歐盟企業生產的產品。碳邊界調整機制（Carbon Border Adjustment Mechanism；簡稱CBAM）就是一個標竿工具，對高碳排的進口產品，以公平的價格鼓勵在非歐盟國家更環保的生產。歐盟逐步對進口產品採行CBAM，同時也要逐步停止對在歐盟境內生產的高碳排產品適用碳排放交易制度（Emission Trading System；簡稱ETS）的免費配額，以支持歐盟的工業進行脫碳。CBAM要確保進口的碳費相當於歐盟境內生產的碳費，而不會削弱歐盟的氣候目標。

　　歐盟的CBAM是全球第一個碳邊界調整機制，也是歐盟氣候政策的重要支柱。CBAM是ETS必然的結果，ETS是全球第一個國際碳排放交易制度與歐盟對抗氣候變遷的旗艦政策（flagship policy）。ETS適用於歐盟境內的製造者，由於適用總量管制與交易（cap and trade）制度，在總量管制下，企業獲得免費的排放配額或必須購買排放憑證。為降低碳排放，2021年7月執委會提出「55套案」（Fit for 55），以落實各項氣候政策與使歐盟成為全球氣候行動領導者，「55套案」改革了一系

列相關的法規，逐步停止ETS的免費配額，並包括了實施CBAM。ETS要求這些歐盟企業應支付排放憑證。執委會體認到加強ETS會造成碳洩漏的現象，由於支付ETS憑證，有些在歐盟市場販售的產品會被在低碳費第三國生產的產品取代，因此對進口產品採行CBAM，可以在進口產品與在歐盟內生產應適用ETS的產品之間，創造一個公平交易的環境。也就是歐盟CBAM規章對特定產品在進口到歐盟關稅領域，建立了一個碳邊界調整機制，以期防止碳洩漏的風險。

高碳排產業有發電廠及發熱、煉油廠、鋼鐵廠、製造鐵、鋁、水泥、造紙及玻璃的工廠、民用航空、船運（自2024年起）。CBAM的設計對電力有特別的規定，因發電有獨特的性質，很難追蹤電子流，CBAM規章第2條第7項與第5條第2項對發電有特別規定。

總而言之，自2023年10月1日起開始啟動CBAM申報義務，也就是2024年1月31日前應進行第一次的申報，這意謂著輸入至歐盟的進口產品，與生產及進口高碳排產品的歐盟企業，應起而行開始準備申報CBAM的各項資料，尤其是應關注後續的發展與開始評價歐盟CBAM法規對其商業活動的影響，而不應只侷限於海關的資料，同時應評估對原、材料來源與供應鏈的衝擊。

2022年12月13日理事會與歐洲議會達成施行新版CBAM的

共識，2023年4月18日歐洲議會完成一讀程序，2023年5月10日完成立法，並於5月16日公布於歐盟官方公報[1]，詳細規定如何申報CBAM的各項程序。重要的內容如下：

一 適用的產品

首先CBAM適用於特定高碳排產品的進口：水泥、鐵及鋼、鋁、肥料、電與氫（附件一）。附件二規定僅考慮直接排放的產品有鐵及鋼、鋁與氫（第7條第1項）。

不適用CBAM的進口產品：（1）每批進口產品的價值低於150歐元；（2）來自第三國的旅客隨身行李的商品低於150歐元；（3）流向或使用於軍事活動的商品。

二 不適用CBAM的國家

進口產品來自適用歐盟ETS、部分適用或完全連結ETS的國家時，不適用CBAM，因此進口產品來自冰島、挪威、列支敦斯登與瑞士不適用歐盟的CBAM。依據CBAM規章第2條第6項規定，第三國與歐盟締結協定完全連結其ETS與歐盟的ETS，此一第三國亦得不適用CBAM。因為北愛爾蘭與愛爾蘭共和國間並無實體的邊界，因此英國亦不適用CBAM。

1　OJ 2023 L 130/52-104.

三 分階段施行CBAM

(一) 自2023年10月1日起，CBAM規章生效施行，逐步對歐盟企業與非歐盟企業適用CBAM，並對公家機關適用CBAM。

(二) 在過渡時期（2023年10月1日－2025年12月31日）（第32條），進口商（係依據2013年第952號歐盟關稅法規章進行海關申報者）必須申報其進口產品內含的溫室氣體（直接與間接排放），尚不需支付碳費或做調整。過渡時期是一個試行階段，對所有利害關係人是一個學習階段，並收集關於內含排放量計算方法的有用資料。

在過渡時期，進口商的申報義務包括：

1. 第33條｜產品進口

(1) 不遲於放行商品自由流通時，海關應告知進口商或第32條情形的間接海關代表人關於第35條的申報義務。

(2) 海關應定期及自動，特別是以2013年第952號共同關稅法規章第56條第5項規定建立的監督機制或以電子資料傳輸方法，告知執委會關於進口產品的資料，包括由歐盟境外加工程序的加工品在內。這些資料包括海關申報人與進口商的EORI號碼、8位的CN碼、數量、原產國、海關申報日期與通關程序。

(3) 執委會應告知海關申報人與進口商設立所在會員國的

主管機關第2項的資料。

2. **第34條│特定關稅程序的申報義務**

(1) 進口2013年第952號共同關稅法規章第256條規定在歐盟境內加工程序的加工產品時,第35條的申報義務應包括關於產品在境內進行加工程序地點與產生進口的加工產品的資料,即便加工產品非本規章附件一的清單產品。本項亦適用於在歐盟境內進行加工程序加工產品在2013年第952號共同關稅法規章第205條規定的退貨情形。

(2) 第35條的申報義務不適用於下列的進口:

　　a. 2013年第952號共同關稅法規章第259條規定在歐盟境外進行加工程序所生產的加工產品;

　　b. 構成2013年第952號共同關稅法規章第205條規定退貨的產品。

3. **第35條│申報義務**

(1) 在日曆年的特定季度進口商品時,第32條規定的進口商、間接海關代表人應對該季度繳交CBAM報告。CBAM報告應包含在該季度的進口產品資料,不遲於該季度結束後一個月繳交給執委會。

(2) CBAM報告應包含下列的資料:

　　a. 以兆瓦時(megawatt-hours,MWh)說明電力及以噸說明其他產品、按每個工廠設施在原產國生產的產

品類型，表述每個類型產品的總量；

b. 以每兆瓦時電力產生的碳排放噸數及以每種產品類型每噸排放的碳排放噸數說明其他產品、依據附件四的計算方法說明實際內含排放的總量；

c. 依據施行法計算第7項的總間接排放量；

d. 在進口產品內含排放量已經在原產國繳交的碳費，考慮所有的扣減或其他形式的補償。

(3) 執委會應定期通知相關的主管機關這些進口商的清單或設立於會員國的間接海關代表人清單，包括有正當理由認為未履行第1項規定繳交CBAM報告的義務。

(4) 執委會認為CBAM報告不完全或不正確時，應通知進口商設立所在會員國的主管機關或第32條規定的情形，間接海關代表人所在會員國的主管機關，應繳交完全或更正報告所需的額外資料。主管機關應啟動更正程序，並通知進口商或第32條規定的情形，間接海關代表人應繳交更正報告所需的額外資料。在適當時，進口商或間接海關代表人應繳交一份更正報告給相關的主管機關與執委會。

(5) 會員國主管機關啟動本條第4項規定的更正程序，包括收到第4項規定的相關資料在內，與決定進口商或第32條規定的情形，間接海關代表人未採取必要步驟更正CBAM報告，或相關的主管機關決定，包括考量第3項規定收到資料在內，進口商或第32條規定的情形，間

接海關代表人未履行第1項規定繳交CBAM報告時,該主管機關應科處進口商或第32條規定的情形,間接海關代表人有效、適當與有勸阻作用的罰金。為此,主管機關應通知進口商或第32條規定的情形,間接海關代表人,並告知執委會下列的事項:

a. 結論與結論的理由、進口商或第32條規定的情形,間接海關代表人未履行繳交季度的CBAM報告或採取必要的步驟更正報告;

b. 科處進口商或第32條規定的情形,間接海關代表人的罰金金額;

c. 罰金自何時生效的日期;

d. 進口商或第32條規定的情形,間接海關代表人應採取行動支付罰金;與

e. 進口商或第32條規定的情形,間接海關代表人申訴的權利。

(6) 在從執委會收到本條規定的資料後,主管機關決定不採取行動時,主管機關應告知執委會。

(7) 授權執委會通過關於下列事務的施行法:

a. 應申報的資料、申報的方法與表格,包括按原產國與產品類型的詳細資料,以支持第2項第a款、第b款與第c款的總量、以及第2項第d款規定任何相關扣減或其他形式補償的例子;

b. 依據第5項規定應科處罰金的指示範圍與考量決定實

際金額的標準，包括不履行報告的嚴重程度與持續的期間。

c. 關於第2項第d款規定的平均碳費按平均匯率換算為外幣的詳細規則；

d. 附件四規定計算方法要素的詳細規則，包括決定生產程序的系統界限、排放係數、工廠設施實際排放的特定值與其分別應用個別產品的特定值、以及規定方法確保數據的可信賴，包括詳細的程度；

e. 在進口產品間接排放申報要件的方法與表格；表格應包括附件一清單表列產品生產時所使用電量、原產國、發電來源與關於該電力的排放係數。

應依據本規章第29條第2項規定的檢驗程序（examination procedure）通過這些施行法。這些施行法應適用本規章第32條規定的過渡時期內進口產品，並在現有的法律基礎上，適用2003年第87號ETS指令的設施。

(三) 在過渡時期，設立於一會員國的進口商依據2013年第952號共同關稅法規章第18條規定，應指定一個間接海關代表人（例如報關行），而該間接海關代表人亦同意，申報義務應適用於該間接海關代表人。非設立於會員國的進口商，申報義務應適用於間接海關代表人。進口商應提出含有CBAM範圍產品資料的CBAM報告（第35條第2項）。報告應於每季結束後一個月前繳交，因此第一個報告應於

2024年1月前繳交。

　　CBAM報告應包含以兆瓦時或噸說明、按照執委會施行法的分類計算出總內含排放量與在原產國對進口產品內含排放量已經支付的任何碳費，並考量扣減或任何形式的補償（第35條）。

(四) 自2024年12月31日起，適用

　　第5條　　申請核准

　　第10條　在第三國營運商與工廠設施的登記

　　第14條　CBAM登記簿

　　第16條　登記簿的帳戶與第17條核准（第36條第2項第a款）

(五) 自2026年1月1日起，適用

　　第2條　　第2項

　　第4條　　產品進口

　　第6條　　CBAM申報

　　第7條　　計算內含的排放量

　　第8條　　內含排放量的查證

　　第9條　　在第三國已經支付的碳費

　　第15條　風險分析

　　第16條　登記簿的帳戶

　　第17條　核准

　　第18條　查證人的認證

第19條　審查CBAM申報

第20條　出售CBAM憑證

第1項　由會員國在由執委會設立的共同中央平台出售憑證。

第3項　在每個工作日結束時，中央平台出售、買回與註銷憑證的資料應移轉給CBAM登記簿。

第4項　以第21條規定的價格出售憑證給經核准的CBAM申報人。

第5項　每張憑證有一個自己的辨識號碼。

第21條　CBAM憑證價格

第22條　繳交CBAM憑證

第23條　買回CBAM憑證

第24條　註銷CBAM憑證

第25條　適用於產品進口的規則

第26條　罰金

第27條　規避

第31條　ETS免費配額與繳交CBAM憑證

進口商必須每季申報前一年進口到歐盟的產品數量與其內含的溫室氣體排放量，進口商必須繳交相當於排放量的憑證數目。CBAM憑證價格為ETS憑證每週平均的拍賣價格（第21條）。

在2026年至2034年逐步停止ETS的免費配額，同時逐步完

全適用CBAM。自2026年以後，CBAM會影響非歐盟的製造業者與所涵蓋產品的供應商、進口商與下游的歐盟產業部門。每季必須申報（1）進口產品的碳排數量；（2）這些進口產品實際的排放量（直接與間接排放）；與（3）在第三國已經支付的碳費（CBAM規章第35條），在產品原產國已經繳交碳費時，可扣減。

在過渡時期，將檢討產品適用範圍的可行性，例如特定的下游產品、在討論時認為應適用CBAM的產品，包括有機化學品和聚合物，以期在2030年以前適用ETS所涵蓋的產品。

歐盟的進口商應向進口的會員國主管機關CBAM登記簿登記產品，應向該會員國的主管機關購買CBAM憑證。新版CBAM規章的核准申請規則更詳細，設立於會員國的進口商在進口適用CBAM的商品前，應申請為合格的CBAM申報人身分。

歐盟的進口商必須申報其進口的碳排放量，每年繳交相當於碳排量的憑證數目。

若進口商可以證明在生產時已經在原產國支付碳費時，可以扣減相當的碳排放量，而少繳CBAM憑證。每季進口商必須申報進口產品的碳排放量、詳細申報直接排放與間接排放、以及在第三國已經繳交的碳費。在過渡時期，若進口商未按季申報或未採取必要措施更正CBAM報告時，進口商會受罰；尚未

明確規定罰金的金額，但是應具有有效、適當與嚇阻作用。

依據CBAM規章第7條第6項規定，執委會應公布施行法，定義CBAM的適用範圍，包括界定生產程序與相關的前體材料、排放係數與默認值（default value）。在過渡時期結束前，針對不同的議題，執委會應提出報告評估是否擴大CBAM的適用範圍（CBAM規章第30條第2項第a款）。

第27條規定，為避免規避，CBAM亦適用於在歐盟境內加工程序所生產的加工產品，這些加工產品亦在歐盟內自由流通（CBAM規章第2條第1項）。在2026年過渡時期結束前，執委會會進行檢討，有可能擴大產品的適用範圍與服務，以避免造成碳洩漏（CBAM規章第30條第2項），新規定擴大規避的情形：

1. 輕微變更產品的稅則稅號（CBAM規章第27條第5項），
2. 人為的分裝運送以受惠於CBAM的例外規定。

自2026年起，應對進口產品收取CBAM費用，計算時依據下列三個要件：

1. 進口產品生產時所造成的碳排放量。排放量的計算包括直接排放量（生產者直接掌控生產所產生的排放量）與間接排放量（指在生產過程中消耗電力、熱氣、冷卻所產生的碳排放量）。在2026年過渡時期結束前，執委會得擴大CBAM憑證適用到間接排放（CBAM規章第

30條第2項）[2]。

2. 每單位的碳價格依據歐盟ETS的碳價計算，也就是ETS憑證等於CBAM憑證價格。

3. 在產品生產時的原產國已經支付的碳費金額得扣減CBAM的費用。

CBAM規章第3條第22項，定義內含的排放量（embedded emissions）包含產品生產時的直接排放與生產程序消耗電力的間接排放，附件四並詳細規定。原則上應繳交CBAM憑證的數目應依據實際的排放量，使用生產程序主要的數據，若無法適用計算實際排放量時，應依據CBAM規章第7條第2項（若無法適當確定實際排放時，運用默認值計算應繳交的CBAM憑證）與附件四規定的默認值計算排放量。按出口國與相關產品的平均排放量確定默認值，仍待確定因增加所造成增多的排放量。未來執委會將報告適用範圍，將會變更適用範圍。

為計算碳排放量，附件四區分簡單產品（simple good）與複雜產品（complex good），簡單產品是指在生產過程只需使用材料（前體）而零碳排的燃料所生產的產品；複雜產品是指其他非簡單產品的產品。附件四第5點規定在進口的電力適用實際內含排放量的條件，若經核准的CBAM申報人符合下列所有

---

2 歐盟係以產品排放量為準，而非如世界商業永續發展理事會（World Business Council of Sustainable Development）的溫室氣體排放分類（範疇1、2與3）的方法。

的標準時，得取代第7條第3項規定的默認值，而適用實際內含排放量計算：

1. 在經核准的CBAM申報人與位於第三國的電力生產者間的購電協議（power purchase agreement）涵蓋了所主張使用實際內含排放量的電量依據附件四規定的方法計算內含的排放量，並依據第7條第7項通過的施行法具體規定；

2. 發電設備是直接連結到歐盟的輸電系統或可顯示在出口時，在發電設備與歐盟輸電系統間的網絡在任何時候無任何實體的網絡擁塞；

3. 發電設施每千瓦時電力的化石燃料未排放超過550g二氧化碳；

4. 所主張使用實際內含排放等量的電量已經明確指定由原產國、目的地國和每個第三過境國（若有關）的所有負責輸電系統營運商分配的互連容量，以及指定容量和由設施同一時段不得超過一小時的電力生產；

5. 由一個認證的查證人證明符合上述的標準。查證人至少每個月收到說明如何履行上述標準的中期報告（intrim report）。也就是在適用電力實際內含排放量時，經核准CBAM申報人應說明直接連結到發電來源或對所申報等量的電力有一個購電協議。購電協議內的累計電量及其相應的實際內含排放量不應算入國家

排放係數或依據第4.3點分別使用於計算產品間接電力內含排放量的二氧化碳排放係數。

6. 對間接排放量適用實際內含排放量的條件：若可顯示在進口產品生產的工廠設施與發電來源間直接的技術連結、或該工廠設施的營運商與位於第三國的電力生產者對相當於所主張一個特定值使用量的電量締結了一個購電協議，經核准CBAM申報人得適用實際內含排放量，取代第7條第7項規定的默認值計算。

7. 依據第7條第2項根據地區個別的特質調整默認值：對特別的區域與在第三國內客觀的排放係數具有特質的地區，得調整默認值。針對特別的地方特性，有可使用經調整的數據，並可確定更多針對性的默認值時，得使用這些默認值。對來自第三國或一群第三國的產品、或在第三國內的一個地區的產品，依據可信賴的數據，申報人得說明替代的區域特別默認值低於由執委會決定的默認值時，得使用這些區域特別默認值。

CBAM的價格係購買應支付碳排放量憑證所支付的價格，CBAM憑證的價格係依據歐盟ETS憑證每個日曆週的拍賣平均價格（CBAM規章第20條第1項與第21條第1項）；依據第21條第3項規定，執委會定義計算CBAM憑證平均價格的特別方法。總而言之，在由執委會設置的共同中央平台出售CBAM憑證，憑證價格應按每個日曆週在歐盟ETS共同拍賣平台收盤平

均價格。

　　進口商在原產國已經支付碳費或碳費，得主張可調整而減少應繳交憑證數目的碳費依據CBAM規章第3條第23項與第9條第1項規定，執委會並得與第三國締結協定，以考慮其碳定價機制，並依據該協定調整碳費（CBAM規章第2條第12項）。

　　自2026年起，應對進口的產品採行下列的行政義務：

1. 申請CBAM涵蓋產品進口的許可，依據CBAM規章第5條與第25條第1項規定，僅得由一會員國的主管機關核准的進口商才得進口受規範的產品，也就是僅由一會員國主管機關核准的CBAM申報人才得進口產品到歐盟關稅領域；受核准的CBAM申報人得代表一個以上的進口商；依據第17條規定，任何人得申請核准進口；經核准後，進口商取得一個為行政用途的CBAM帳戶（即應在進口的會員國開設CBAM帳戶）。執委會應確保所有的憑證有一個專屬的身分號碼，在憑證購買後，應登記到CBAM申報人的帳戶（第20條）。

2. 依據CBAM規章第3條第18項與第20條規定，進口商應向會員國的主管機關購買受規範產品生產每噸排放量的CBAM憑證。自購買日起，CBAM憑證的效期為二年。與ETS憑證不同，進口商彼此間不得交易CBAM憑證，但得以購買憑證時的價格繳回主管機關；每年7月

1日以前，執委會應註銷進口商在先前購買但仍然在經核准CBAM申報人在登記簿的CBAM憑證，無任何賠償註銷這些CBAM憑證（第24條）。

3. 在提出CBAM申報前，進口商必須確保由一位經認證的查證人查證排放的總量（第8條）。經認證的查證者應出具一份查證影本。也就是經申報的內含排放量必須由一位獨立的經認證查證人的查證。

4. 每年5月31日前，經核准CBAM申報人應提出前一日曆年的CBAM申報，依據CBAM規章第6條規定，說明受規範產品進口以兆瓦時或噸說明的總碳排放量、直接排放量與符合排放量的CBAM數目（已經扣減在原產國支付的碳費與調整ETS的免費配額）。

5. 每年5月31日前，經核准CBAM申報人應繳交相當於在前一日曆年進口產品排放量的CBAM憑證總數目，但依據第31條規定CBAM憑證數目得按ETS免費配額的範圍做調整，依據修訂的ETS規定，在2025年至2035年間逐步停止免費配額。在5月31日前，未繳交CBAM憑證時，申報人會被科處罰金，並得依據消費者價格提高罰金（第26條）。若非由經核准的CBAM申報人進口受規範產品時，罰金可提高三倍至五倍，完全取決於未遵循的期間、嚴重程度、範圍、意圖的性質與重複累犯情形、調查時企業的配合度（第26條第2項）。在未遵循的情形，仍應購買與繳交所需的CBAM憑證數

目，再加上應支付的罰金。

在提出申報後的4年內，主管機關得審查CBAM申報；在必要時，亦會適當調整CBAM憑證的數目，檢查得在進口商營業所進行稽核；進口商得申訴主管機關的決定（第19條）。

依據ETS指令第10a條第1a項規定降低免費配額的計算：

年度	免費配額的降低係數
2026	97.5%
2027	95%
2028	90%
2029	77.5%
2030	51.5%
2031	39%
2032	26.5%
2033	14%
2034	0%

CBAM是防止碳洩漏風險與支持歐盟對抗氣候變遷的重要措施，同時確保WTO規則，以防止形成新的保護措施。實際上，美國加州已經對電力進口實施CBAM。歐盟的CBAM規章有很大的影響力，各國亦跟進立法：

1. 台灣氣候變遷因應法（2022/01/22）
2. 美國Clean Competition Act，適用25個產業，例如石

油、天然氣、化學肥料、鐵及鋼、玻璃與造紙等，碳價每噸55美元，並逐年增加。

3. 加拿大與日本也正規劃採行CBAM。

國際貨幣基金（IMF）與經濟合作暨發展組織（OECD），最近亦進行研究CBAM措施應如何支持國際努力以降低溫室氣體的排放；值得一提的是，2021年7月9日至10日的G20財政部長會議，亦強調應更緊密進行國際協調運用碳定價機制與在G7[3]創立一個氣候俱樂部（Climate Club）。2020年12月歐盟的預算及自主財源協議規定CBAM成為歐盟的自主財源，是歐盟預算的收入。CBAM已經是國際趨勢，已經是一個重要的氣候措施。

非歐盟的製造者應通報在歐盟境內的進口商關於適用CBAM產品內含排放量的資訊，進口至歐盟時，若無提供產品的資訊時，歐盟的進口商得適用每個產品碳排放量的默認值而確定應購買的CBAM憑證數目，除非在和解程序中，進口商得說明實際排放量，而依規定繳交相當數目的CBAM憑證。受CBAM規章規範的台灣產業應立即行動準備2023年10月施行的CBAM報告：

1. 盤點出口產品的稅則稅號是否是CBAM的適用範圍；

3　G7為七大工業大國高峰會議，包括日本、美國、加拿大、英國、法國、德國與義大利。

2. 檢討目前溫室氣體的計算方法、評估每個產品的碳排放是否夠詳細與方法是否可以符合CBAM的要求；

3. 對智慧碳排計算，是否可依據現有系統提供CBAM所需的數據；

4. 發展準備CBAM報告的路徑，考量上述的步驟，得包含發展或更新溫室氣體的計算方法、發展內部的程序、選擇及實施智慧碳排執行試運行報告。

台灣廠商進口CBAM產品到歐盟的申報時程歸納如下：

過渡時期：自2023年10月1日至2025年12月31日止

進口商或其海關代表人應每季向執委會提出CBAM產品申報；

第一個季度申報必須在2024年1月1日前提出，到期日為2024年4月30日；

第一個季度報告應涵蓋2023年10月1日至12月31日期間的資料；

申報內容為進口產品數量、產品的直接及間接排放、在原產國已經支付的碳費與產生的補償。

自2024年1月1日起

第5條申請核准；

第10條在第三國營運商與工廠設施的登記；

第14條CBAM登記簿；

第16條登記簿的帳戶與第17條核准（第36條第2項第a款）。

自2026年1月1日起

開始年度報告，首次年度申報到期日為2027年5月31日；

進口商應取得CBAM憑證數目相當於自產品製造產生的排放量；

每年應向執委會提出CBAM申報，應含有前一個日曆年進口產品內含排放總量與應繳交的CBAM憑證數目；

開始購買CBAM憑證。

PART 2

CBAM 規章
中文翻譯

主題事務、適用範圍與定義

第1條 | 主題事務

1. 本規章建立一個碳邊界調整機制（CBAM）以表示附件一清單表列產品進口到歐盟關稅領域的內含溫室氣體排放，以期防止碳洩漏的風險，因而降低全球碳排放與支持巴黎協定的目標，並對在第三國營運商創造排放降低的誘因。

2. 藉由適用本規章第2條規定的產品進口到歐盟關稅領域的一套等值規則，CBAM補充在2003年第87號指令在歐盟境內建立的溫室氣體排放許可交易制度。

3. 規定CBAM取代2003年第87號指令建立的機制，以防止回應該指令第10a條規定歐盟ETS免費配額的碳洩漏風險。

第2條 | 適用範圍

1. 本規章適用於來自第三國在附件一清單表列的產品，而這些第三國產品或從依據2013年第952號共同關稅法規章第256條規定這些產品在境內進行加工程序產生的加工品進口到歐盟關稅領域。

2. 本規章亦適用於本規章來自第三國附件一清單表列的產品，而這些第三國產品依據2013年第952號共同關稅

法規章第256條規定這些產品在境內進行加工程序產生的加工品運送到歐盟關稅領域相鄰會員國的大陸礁層或專屬經濟區內的人工島、固定或浮動結構、或任何其他結構。

執委會應公布施行法，詳細規定適用CBAM於這些產品的條件，特別是針對等同於進入歐盟關稅領域和放行自由流通的概念、關於提出這些產品的CBAM申報與由海關進行檢查的程序。應依據本規章第29條第2項規定的檢驗程序，公布這些施行法。

3. 以逐漸不適用第1項與第2項規定的方式，本規章不適用於：

   (a) 進口本規章附件一清單表列的產品至歐盟關稅領域，而這些產品的內在值每批不超過2009年第1186號規章第23條規定輕微價值產品具體的價值；

   (b) 來自第三國的旅客隨身行李含有的產品，而這些產品的內在值不超過2009年第1186號規章第23條規定輕微價值產品具體的價值；

   (c) 依據2015年第2446號執委會授權規章第1條第49款流入或使用於軍事活動的產品。

4. 以逐漸不適用第1項與第2項規定的方式，本規章不應適用於源自附件三第1點表列的第三國與領域。

5. 依據2013年第952號規章第59條規定的非優惠原產地規則，應認為源自於第三國的進口產品。

6. 附件三第1點表列的第三國與領域符合所有下列的條件：

    (a) 歐盟ETS適用於該第三國或領域、或該第三國或領域與歐盟締結了一個協議完全連結歐盟ETS至該第三國或領域的排放交易制度；

    (b) 在產品原產國對該產品的溫室氣體內含排放量，而無任何超過適用歐盟ETS的扣減已經有效支付過的碳費。

7. 若一第三國或領域的電力市場，透過市場連結而納入歐盟單一電力市場，且自該第三國或領域進口電力至歐盟關稅領域適用CBAM無技術解決方案，自該第三國或領域的電力進口應不適用CBAM，在執委會評估過已經符合第8項規定的下列所有條件：

    (a) 第三國或領域與歐盟締結了一個規定在電力應適用歐盟法的協議，包括發展再生能源的立法、以及在能源、環境與競爭領域的其他規則；

    (b) 在該第三國或領域的國內立法施行歐盟電力市場立法的主要規定，包括發展再生能源與電力市場的市場連結；

    (c) 第三國或領域已經提出一個路徑圖給執委會，路徑圖含有採取措施施行第d款與第e款規定條件的時間表；

    (d) 第三國或領域已經承諾在2050年以前氣候中和，在

歐盟CBAM法規：台灣廠商因應之道與申報準備

適用時，因而正式表述與告知聯合國氣候變遷架構公約（UNFCCC）一個在本世紀中期、長期低溫室氣體排放發展具氣候中和目標的策略，並在其國內立法施行該承諾；

(e) 施行第c款規定路徑圖的第三國或領域已經表述履行其規定的截止期限與實質進展在基於該路徑圖的氣候行動領域邁向連結歐盟法至國內法，包括邁向在等值的水準，在歐盟特別是關於發電的碳定價在內；以等同於歐盟ETS的價格，在2030年1月1日以前完成施行電力的排放交易制度；

(f) 第三國或領域採行一個有效制度，防止自其他不履行第a款至第e款規定條件的第三國或領域間接進口電力至歐盟。

8. 履行第7項規定條件的第三國或領域應列入附件三第2點的清單，且應提出二個履行這些條件的報告，第一個報告在2025年7月1日前與第二個報告在2027年12月31日前提出。在2025年12月31日前與在2028年7月1日前，特別是基於第7項第c款規定的路徑圖與自第三國或領域收到的報告，執委會應評估第三國或領域持續履行第7項規定的條件。

9. 第三國或領域適用下列一個或數個條件時，應自附件三第2點清單移除表列的第三國或領域：

(a) 執委會有理由認為該第三國或領域未展現充分的進

展遵循第7項規定的一個條件、或該第三國或領域已經採取不符合歐盟氣候與環境法規目標的行動；

(b) 第三國或領域已經採取違反其脫碳目標的步驟，例如提供公共補助設立排放自每千瓦時電力化石燃料550g二氧化碳的新發電容量；

(c) 執委會有證據顯示提高出口電力至歐盟的結果、在該第三國或領域發電每千瓦時的排放量，與2026年1月1日相比，至少增加5%。

10. 依據第28條規定，授權執委會公布授權法，以期補充本規章，規定已經自附件三第2點清單移除第三國或領域的要件與程序、確保針對電力適用本規章於這些第三國或領域。若在這種情形，市場連結仍不符合本規章的適用時，執委會得決定自歐盟的市場連結排除第三國或領域，且要求在歐盟與這些第三國或領域間邊界的明確容量分配，以期可以適用CBAM。

11. 依據第28條規定，授權執委會公布授權法，以期以增加或移除第三國或領域，修訂附件三第1點或第2點表列第三國或領域的清單，取決於在該第三國或領域是否履行本條第6項、第7項或第9項規定的條件。

12. 針對考慮在這些國家或領域的碳定價機制，為適用第9條的目的，歐盟得與第三國或領域締結協議。

第3條│定義規定

為本規章之目的，適用下列的定義：

(1) 產品係指附件一清單表列的產品；

(2) 溫室氣體係指在附件一針對該附件清單表列每個產品具體表列的溫室氣體；

(3) 排放係指從產品生產釋出溫室氣體到大氣層；

(4) 進口係指2013年第952號共同關稅法規章第201條通關放行自由流通；

(5) 歐盟碳排放交易制度係指2003年第87號指令附件一清單表列的活動，但不包括航空活動，在歐盟境內的溫室氣體排放許可的制度；

(6) 歐盟關稅領域係指2013年第952號規章第4條定義的領域；

(7) 第三國係指歐盟關稅領域外的國家或領域；

(8) 大陸礁層係指聯合國海洋法公約第76條定義的大陸礁層；

(9) 專屬經濟區係指聯合國海洋法公約第55條定義的專屬經濟區，且由一會員國依據該公約宣布為專屬經濟區；

(10) 內在值係指2015年第2446號授權規章第1條第48款定義的商品內在值；

(11) 市場連結係指透過歐盟系統分配輸電容量，同時符合2015年第1222號規章規定訂單與分配跨區域的容量；

(12) 明確的容量分配係指從電力交易分開，跨境輸電容量的分配；

(13) 主管機關係指依據第11條由每個會員國指定的機關；

(14) 海關係指2013年第952號規章第5條第1款定義的會員國海關；

(15) 進口商係指以自己的姓名且為自己的利益，進行報關放行商品自由流通的人、或依據2013年第952號規章第18條規定由間接的海關代表人進行報關，此一報關係為其利益者；

(16) 海關申報人係指2013年第952號規章第5條第15款定義的申報人以自己的姓名或在此一報關以其姓名者進行報關放行商品自由流通；

(17) 經核准的CBAM申報人係指第17條規定由主管機關核准的人；

(18) 人係指自然人或法人、或非法人但歐盟法或會員國法承認其有法律行為能力的人合協會（association of persons）。

(19) 設立於一會員國係指：

　　(a) 在自然人的情形，在一會員國有居所的任何人；

　　(b) 在法人或人合協會的情形，在一會員國有登記的辦公室、中央的總部或永久營業設立的任何人；

(20) 經濟營運商登記與身份號碼（EORI號碼）係指依據2013年第952號規章第9條為關稅目的進行登記，由海

關核發的號碼；

(21) 直接排放係指自產品生產過程的排放，包括在生產過程消耗熱氣及冷卻，從生產熱氣及冷卻的排放，而不問熱氣或冷卻的生產地點；

(22) 內含排放量係指在產品生產期間釋出的直接排放與在生產產品所消耗電力在生產電力的間接排放，依據附件四規定的公式與依據第7條第7項公布的施行法所規定的方法計算；

(23) CO_2e噸係指一公噸的CO_2e或有等值全球暖化的潛力在附件一清單表列任何其他溫室氣體的量；

(24) CBAM憑證係指相當於產品內含排放一噸CO_2e以電子形式的憑證；

(25) 繳交係指對進口的產品所申報的內含排放量或對應已經申報的進口產品內含排放量的CBAM憑證抵銷；

(26) 生產過程係指在一個設施生產產品進行的化學及物理程序；

(27) 默認值（default value）係指自產品內含排放量的間接數據（secondary data）所計算或推論的數值；

(28) 實際排放量係指基於自產品生產過程直接數據（primary data）與自在這些生產過程消耗電力，在附件四規定計算公式確定的電力生產，所計算出的排放量；

(29) 碳費係指在第三國已支付的金額，在一個碳排放降低制度，以租稅、徵收或費用形式或在溫室氣體排放交

易制度下，以排放許可的形式，依據由這樣一個措施
所涵蓋的溫室氣體計算在產品生產時排放；

(30) 設施係指進行生產過程的一個固定的技術實體；

(31) 營運商係指在第三國營運或掌控一設施的任何人；

(32) 國家的認證機構係指依據2008年第765號規章第4條第
1項規定[4]，由每個會員國指定的國家認證機構；

(33) 歐盟ETS許可（配額）係指針對2003年第87號指令附
件一清單表列的活動，但不包括航空活動，2003年第
87號指令第3條第a款定義的許可；

(34) 間接排放係指在產品生產過程消耗的電力，自該電力
生產的排放，而不問所消耗電力的生產地點。

經核准CBAM申報人的義務與權利

第4條｜產品的進口

應僅由經核准CBAM申報人進口產品至歐盟關稅領域。

第5條｜核准之申請

1. 在進口產品至歐盟關稅領域前，設立於一會員國的進
   口商應申請經核准CBAM申報人的身份（申請核准）。

---

4 每個會員國應指定一個單一的國家認證機構。

在此一進口商依據2013年第952號規章第18條規定指定一位間接的海關代表人，且間接的海關代表人同意擔任經核准CBAM申報人時，間接海關代表人應提出核准的申請。

2. 在進口商非設立於一會員國時，間接海關代表人應提出核准的申請。

3. 應透過第14條規定的CBAM登記簿提出申請核准。

4. 以逐步不適用第1項規定的方式，在透過明確分配容量分配電力進口的輸電容量時，為本規章之目的，分配其進口容量且指定該進口容量者應視為是在海關申報已經申報電力進口的會員國經核准的CBAM申報人。

在同一小時每個邊界不再超過一個小時且無出口或過境扣除的期限，應可能量測進口。

在進行海關申報的會員國主管機關應在CBAM登記簿登記這個人。

5. 申請核准應包括關於申請人的下列資料：

(a) 姓名、地址與聯絡資料；

(b) EORI號碼；

(c) 在歐盟境內進行的主要經濟活動；

(d) 在申請人所在會員國的稅務機關出具申請人無欠稅證明；

(e) 誠實聲明，即申請人在提出申請的年度前五年間無重大違反或累犯違反關稅法、租稅規章或市場濫用

規則，包括無重大經濟犯罪的前科在內；

(f) 說明申請人履行本規章義務財務及營運能力的必要資料、與主管機關基於風險評估決定支持確認該資料的文件，例如關帳的最近三個會計年度損益表與資產負債表；

(g) 按產品類型、提出申請的日曆年與下一個日曆年，產品進口到歐盟關稅領域的估計金額與數量；

(h) 若適用時，申請人為其利益者的姓名與聯絡資料。

6. 申請人得隨時撤回申請。

7. 經核准的CBAM申報人透過CBAM登記簿，這些資料變更會影響該決定或所給予核准的內容，應立即通知主管機關所提供本條第5項規定的資料在給予第17條經核准CBAM申報人身份決定後資料的任何變更。

8. 授權執委會公布施行法，規定申請人、主管機關與執委會間的溝通往來、申請核准的標準格式與透過CBAM登記簿提出此一申請的程序、主管機關應遵循的程序與本條第1項規定的處理申請核准的截止期限、以及主管機關辨別電力進口的經核准CBAM申報人規則。應依據第29條第2項規定的檢驗程序，公布這些施行法。

第6條 │ CBAM申報

1. 在每年5月31日以前，且首次在2027年對2026年，每位

經核准CBAM申報人應使用第14條規定的CBAM登記簿對前一個日曆年提出CBAM申報。

2. CBAM申報應含有下列的資料：

   (a) 在前一個日曆年間進口產品的每種類型總量，以每兆瓦時表示電力與以噸表示其他產品；

   (b) 依據第7條計算與依據第8條查證本項第a款產品的內含排放量，以每兆瓦時電力的碳排放噸數表示或每噸每種類型產品的碳排放噸數表示；

   (c) 應繳交的CBAM憑證總數，在扣除第9條在第三國已經支付的碳費與反應第31條規定歐盟ETS免費配額做必要的調整後，相當於本項第b款的內含排放量；

   (d) 依據第8條與附件六規定，由經認證的查證人核發查證報告的影本。

3. 依據2013年第952號規章第256條規定從在歐盟境內進行的加工程序產生的加工品為進口，經核准CBAM申報人應在CBAM申報報告在境內加工程序與產生進口加工品的產品內含排放量，即便是加工品非本規章附件一清單表列的產品。本項規定亦應適用於從境內加工程序產生的加工品是2013年第952號規章第205條規定的退貨。

4. 本規章附件一清單表列的進口產品是從依據2013年第952號規章第259條規定境外加工程序產生的加工品，

經核准CBAM申報人應在CBAM申報僅報告在歐盟關稅領域外進行加工營運的排放量。

5. 進口產品是2013年第952號規章第203條規定的退貨時，經核准CBAM申報人應在CBAM報告分開申報，對這些產品的內含排放總量為「零」。

6. 授權執委會公布施行法，規定CBAM申報的標準格式，包括對每個設施、原產國與產品類型應申報的詳細資料，這些資料支持本條第2項規定的全部，特別是針對內含排放量與已支付的碳費、透過CBAM登記簿提出CBAM申報的程序、與安排本條第2項第c款、依據第22條第1項規定的繳交CBAM憑證，尤其是針對經核准CBAM申報人繳交憑證的程序與挑選。應依據第29條第2項規定的檢驗程序，公布施行法。

第7條｜內含排放量之計算

1. 產品的內含排放量應依據附件四規定的公式計算。對附件二清單表列的產品，應僅計算與考慮直接排放。

2. 電力以外的其他產品，應依據附件四第2點與第3點規定的公式得出的實際排放量確定他他產品的內含排放量。在無法適當確定實際排放量時、以及在間接排放量的情形，應參考附件四第4.1.點規定的公式得出的默認值，確定內含排放量。

3. 應參考附件四第4.2點規定的公式得出的默認值確定進

口電力的內含排放量，但經核准CBAM申報人說明確定的標準符合基於附件四第5點列示的實際排放的內含排放量，不在此限。

4. 應依據附件四第4.3點規定的公式與依據本條第7項公布的施行法具體規定，計算內含間接排放量，但經核准CBAM申報人說明確定的標準符合基於附件四第6點列示的實際排放的內含排放量，不在此限。

5. 經核准CBAM申報人應保存計算附件五規定要件的內含排放量所需資料的記錄。這些記錄應充分詳細使依據第18條認證的查證人可以查證第8條與附件六規定的內含排放量，且執委會與主管機關可以依據第19條第2項審查CBAM報告。

6. 至提出或應提出CBAM申報的年度後第四年結束時止，經核准CBAM申報人應保存第5項規定資料的記錄，包括查證人的報告在內。

7. 授權執委會針對下列事項公布施行法：

   (a) 適用附件四規定的計算公式要素，包括確定生產過程及相關投入材料（前體）、排放係數、實際排放量設施具體值的系統界限、默認值及其分別適用於個別產品、以及規定基於應確定默認值確保數據可靠的方法，包括數據詳細的程度與查證在內，並包括更進一步規定附件四第1點視為「簡單產品」與「複雜產品」的產品特性；這些施行法亦應具體規

定認為實際排放量無法適當確定的條件、以及說明所需標準正當化為第2項之目的其他產品內含排放量符合附件四清單表列第5點與第6點使用在產品生產程序消耗電力的實際排放量證據的要素；與

(b) 依據附件四第4.3點適用第4項規定計算公式的要素。

在客觀上正當合理時，第一段的施行法應規定可以依據特別區域、地區或國家考慮影響排放特別的客觀要素，例如主要能源或工業過程，調整默認值。這些施行法應以現行的排放監測及查證的法規與2003年第87號指令涵蓋的設施活動數據為基礎，特別是2018年第2066號執委會施行規章、2018年第2067號施行規章與2019年第331號執委會授權規章。應依據第29條第2項規定的檢驗程序，公布施行法。

第8條 ｜ 內含排放量之查證

1. 經核准CBAM申報人應確保在依據第6條規定提出CBAM申報所申報的內含排放總量，基於附件六規定的查證原則，經由一位依據第18條規定認證的查證人查證。

2. 對於依據第10條規定在第三國設施所生產產品的內含排放量，經核准CBAM申報人得選擇使用認證第10條第7項規定應揭露的資料，以履行本條第1項的義務。

3. 授權執委會公布施行法，針對下列事項，規定附件六規定的查證原則：

    (a) 在正當理由的情況下，在不危及對內含排放量可靠估計的情況下，有可能免除查證人參觀生產相關產品設施（查廠）的義務；

    (b) 對決定錯誤陳述或不合規是否重大的門檻值定義；

    (c) 對查證報告所需的支持文件，包括其格式在內。

第9條 ｜ 在第三國已支付的碳費

1. 經核准CBAM申報人得在CBAM申報主張減少應繳交CBAM憑證的數目，以期考慮已經在原產國對所申報內含排放量已支付碳費。僅在碳費已經在原產國有效支付碳費時，才得主張扣減。在這種情形，應考慮該國可能導致碳費降低的任何扣減或其他形式的補償。

2. 經核准CBAM申報人應保存說明所申報內含排放量針對第1項規定已經在產品原產國有效支付碳費所需文件的記錄。經核准CBAM申報人應特別保存關於任何扣減或其他形式補償可使用的證據，特別是參考該國相關的立法。在該文件含有的資料應由獨立於經核准CBAM申報人與原產國相關的人士認證。該獨立認證人士的姓名與聯絡資料應出現在文件上。經核准CBAM申報人亦應保存實際支付碳費的證據。

3. 至CBAM申報提出或應提出年度期間後第四年結束時

止，經核准CBAM申報人亦應保存第2項規定的記錄。

4. 關於第1項規定已經支付的年度平均碳費轉換為相當的扣減應繳交CBAM憑證數目，包括以外國貨幣已經支付的碳費轉換為歐元的年度平均匯率在內、實際支付碳費所需的證據、本條第1項規定的任何相關扣減或其他形式補償的例子、本條第2項規定獨立人士的資格與確定該人士獨立的條件。應依據第29條第2項規定的檢驗程序，公布這些施行法。

第10條｜在第三國營運商與設施之登記

1. 基於位於第三國的設施營運商之請求，執委會在第14條規定的CBAM登記簿登記該營運商與其設施。

2. 請求第1項規定的登記應含有下列包括登記於CBAM登記簿的資料：

   (a) 營運商的姓名、地址與聯絡資料；

   (b) 每個設施的地點，包括完整地址與以六位小數經緯度的地理座標在內；

   (c) 設施主要的經濟活動。

3. 執委會應通知營運商在CBAM登記簿的登記。自登記通知設施營運商的日期起生效，效期五年。

4. 在登記後第2項規定的資料有任何變更，營運商應立即通知執委會，執委會應在CBAM登記簿立即更新相關的資料。

5. 營運商應：

(a) 依據附件四規定的公式計算，以在本條第1項規定的設施生產的產品類型，確定內含排放量；

(b) 確保本項第a款規定的內含排放量依據附件六規定的查證原則由一位依據第18條規定經認證的查證人查證；

(c) 查證報告影本、以及依據附件五規定計算產品內含排放量所需資料的記錄，在進行查證後，保存四年期限。

6. 本條第5項第c款規定的記錄應充分詳細可以依據第8條與附件六查證內含排放量，且可以依據第19條規定審查由經核准CBAM申報人依據本條第7項應揭露資料所做的CBAM申報。

7. 營運商得向經核准CBAM申報人揭露本條第5項規定查證內含排放量的資料。經核准CBAM申報人應有權使用該揭露的資料，以期履行第8條規定的義務。

8. 營運商得隨時要求自CBAM登記簿註銷。基於此一請求，在通知主管機關後，執委會應註銷營運商，若這些資料非審查提出的CBAM申報所必要時，並應自CBAM登記簿刪除該營運商與其設施。在給予相關營運商聽證機會與諮商相關主管機關後，若執委會發現該營運商的資料不再正確時，執委會亦得註銷資料。執委會應通知主管機關這些註銷。

主管機關

第11條｜主管機關

1. 每個會員國應指定執行本規章規定的作用與職務的主
   管機關，並將其告知執委會。

   執委會應提供給會員國一個所有主管機關的清單，並
   在歐盟官方公報公告該資訊與在CBAM登記簿可取得
   該資訊。

2. 主管機關應交流任何重要或關於本規章執行其作用與
   職務的資訊。

第12條｜執委會

除本規章執行的職務外，執委會應協助主管機關執行本規
章規定的作用與職務，且以支持交流在本規章適用範圍的
最佳實務與公布守則、以促進適當交流資料、在主管機關
彼此間合作及在主管機關與執委會間的合作，應協調主管
機關的活動。

第13條｜專業祕密與資訊揭露

1. 在執行職務時，由主管機關或執委會取得所有性質上
   是機密或基於機密提供的資料，應遵守專業祕密的義
   務。未經提供資料的人或機關明確的事前同意或因歐

盟法或會員國法規定，主管機關或執委會不應揭露這些資料。

2. 以逐步不適用第1項規定的方式，為確保本規章有義務遵循者與適用關稅法，主管機關與執委會得互相分享、分享海關、行政或刑事執行機關與歐洲檢察官辦公室這些資料。這些分享的資料應遵守專業秘密的義務，除歐盟法或會員國法規定外，不應揭露給其他人或機關。

第14條 | CBAM登記簿

1. 執委會應以規格化的電子資料庫形式，設置經核准CBAM申報人的CBAM登記簿，含有這些經核准CBAM申報人的CBAM憑證資料。執委會應使海關與主管機關自動與即時可取得在CBAM登記簿的資料。

2. 第1項規定的CBAM登記簿應含有關於每位經核准CBAM申報人帳戶的資料，特別是

   (a) 經核准CBAM申報人的姓名、地址與聯絡資料；

   (b) 經核准CBAM申報人的EORI號碼；

   (c) CBAM帳號；

   (d) 每位經核准CBAM申報人CBAM憑證的辨識號碼、出售價格、出售日期、與繳交、買回或註銷日期。

3. 登記簿以分開的段落，CBAM登記簿應含有第10條第2項規定在第三國營運商與設施登記的資料。

4. 關於第2項與第3項規定的CBAM登記簿資料應是機密的，但不包括在第三國營運商與設施的姓名、地址與聯絡資料。營運商得選擇不公開其姓名、地址與聯絡資料。執委會應以可相互操作的格式供取得在登記簿公開的資料。

5. 執委會應以每年為基礎公布在附件一清單表列的每個產品在進口產品加總的內含排放量。

6. 執委會應公布施行法，以規範基本規定、特別程序與CBAM登記簿的程序，包括第15條的風險分析、本條第2項與第3項規定電子資料庫含有的資料、第16條規定在CBAM登記簿的帳戶資料、第20條規定傳遞出售、買回與註銷CBAM憑證資料到CBAM登記簿與第25條第3項規定的資料交叉檢查。應依據第29條第2項規定的檢驗程序，公布這些施行法。

第15條 │ 風險分析

1. 對第14條CBAM登記簿記錄的資料與交易，執委會應進行以風險為基礎的檢查，以確保在購買、持有、繳交、買回與註銷CBAM憑證無違規的情事。

2. 若執委會進行第1項的檢查後，發現違規時，應通知相關的主管機關，以便進行進一步的調查，以期更正所確認的違規情事。

第16條│CBAM登記簿的帳戶

1. 執委會核發給每位經核准CBAM申報人一個獨有的CBAM帳號。

2. 應授權每位經核准CBAM申報人進入其CBAM登記簿的帳戶。

3. 執委會應設立帳戶及盡可能給予第17條第1項規定的核准，且應通知經核准的CBAM申報人。

4. 若經核准CBAM申報人已經停止其經濟活動或已經撤銷其核准時，在經核准CBAM申報人已經遵循本規章的所有義務時，執委會應關閉該經核准CBAM申報人的帳戶。

第17條│核准

1. 依據第5條規定提出核准申請時，在符合本條第2項規定的標準時，申請人設立所在會員國的主管機關應給予核准CBAM申報人的身分。

   在給予核准CBAM申報人的身分前，透過CBAM登記簿，主管機關應就核准申請進行諮商程序。諮商程序應包含其他會員國的主管機關與執委會，且不應超過15個工作日。

2. 給予核准CBAM申報人身分應符合下列的標準：

   (a) 針對關稅法、租稅規則、市場濫用規則、或本規章與在本規章公布的授權法及施行法，申請人無重大

違反或累犯情事，特別是在提出申請前五年間，就其經濟活動申請人無重大犯罪行為；

(b) 申請人說明履行本規章義務的財務與營運能力；

(c) 在申請人所在會員國提出申請；

(d) 依據2013年第952號規章第9條規定已經核發給申請人EORI號碼。

3. 主管機關發現不符合本條第2項規定的標準時、或申請人未提供第5條第5項規定列舉的資料時，應拒絕給予核准CBAM申報人的身分。這種拒絕核准CBAM申報人身分的決定應說明拒絕的理由與包括得申訴的資訊。

4. 主管機關給予核准CBAM申報人身分的決定應登記於CBAM登記簿，並應含有下列的資料：

(a) 經核准CBAM申報人的姓名、地址與聯絡資料；

(b) 經核准CBAM申報人的EORI號碼；

(c) 依據第16條第1項規定核發給經核准CBAM申報人CBAM帳號；

(d) 依據本條第5項規定所需的擔保。

5. 為遵循本條第2項第b款規定的標準，若申請人在依據第5條第1項規定提出申請前的完整二個會計年度未設立時，主管機關應要求提供擔保。

主管機關應規定此一擔保金額，按經核准CBAM申報人依據第22條規定針對第5條第5項第g款規定的產品進口應繳交CBAM憑證數目且加總的價格計算金額。應

以由在歐盟境內經營的金融機構見票即付的銀行保證或提供等值保證的其他形式保證，提供擔保。

6. 主管機關確定所提供的擔保不確保或不再足以確保經核准CBAM申報人履行本規章義務的財務與營運能力時，應要求經核准CBAM申報人在提供額外保證（擔保）或依據第5項規定以新的擔保取代原始擔保間做選擇。

7. 在經核准CBAM申報人已經依據第22條繳交CBAM憑證第二年的5月31日後，主管機關應立即解除擔保。

8. 有下列情事時，主管機關應撤銷核准CBAM申報人的身分：

   (a) 經核准CBAM申報人請求撤銷；或

   (b) 經核准CBAM申報人不再符合本條第2項或第6項規定的標準、或已經重大違反或累犯第22條第1項規定繳交CBAM憑證的義務或第22條第2項規定在每個季度結束時在CBAM登記簿的帳戶確保足夠CBAM憑證數目的義務。

   在撤銷核准CBAM申報人身份前，主管機關應給予經核准CBAM申報人聽證的機會，且應針對可能撤銷此一身份進行諮商程序。諮商程序應包含其他會員國的主管機關與執委會，且不應超過15個工作日。

   撤銷決定應含有決定的理由、以及申訴權的資訊。

9. 主管機關應在CBAM登記簿登記下列的資料：

    (a) 申請核准遭第3項規定拒絕的申請人；與

    (b) 依據第8項經撤銷經核准CBAM申報人身分者。

10. 執委會應公布施行法，規定下列的事項：

    (a) 本條第2項規定標準的適用，包括本條第2項第a款規定未重大違反或累犯在內；

    (b) 本條第5項、第6項與第7項規定的擔保適用；

    (c) 本條第8項重大違反或累犯標準的適用；

    (d) 本條第8項撤銷核准CBAM申報人身份的前因後果；與

    (e) 本條第1項與第8項規定諮商程序具體的截止日期與形式。

    應依據第29條第2項規定的檢驗程序，公布第一段的施行法。

第18條｜查證人的認證

1. 為本規章的目的，依據2018年第2067號對相關活動類別施行規章經認證的任何人應為經認證的查證人。授權執委會公布施行法，以提供為本規章目的執行查證所必要的認證查證人的資格與認證證書中的相關活動類別醫治，以辨別相關的活動類別。應依據本規章第29條第2項規定的檢驗程序，公布這些施行法。

2. 依請求，會員國的國家認證機構得認證一人為查證

人，依據所提交的文件，認為係為本規章之目的，在執行第8條與第10條規定的內含排放查證工作時，由此人有能力適用在附件四規定的查核原則。

3. 授權執委會依據第28條規定公布授權法，以期藉由具體化第2項規定給予認證、檢查及監督認證的查證人、撤回認證、相互承認與認證機構同儕評鑑的條件，補充本規章。

第19條｜審查CBAM申報

1. 在審查CBAM申報上，執委會應扮演監督角色。

2. 在應提出CBAM申報年度後第四年結束期間內，依據審查策略，執委會得審查CBAM申報。

   審查得稽核在CBAM申報提供的資料與基於依據第25條由海關通報資料的查證報告、任何其他相關證據，基於認為必要的稽核，包括在經核准CBAM申報人的場所。

   透過CBAM登記簿，執委會應通報CBAM申報人設立所在會員國的主管機關審查的啟動與結果。

   經核准CBAM申報人設立所在會員國的主管機關在本項第一段規定的期間內，亦得審查CBAM申報。透過CBAM登記簿，主管機關應通報執委會審查的啟動與結果。

3. 執委會應定期擬定特別的風險要素與注意事項，基於

針對在歐盟層級施行CBAM的風險分析、考慮在CBAM登記簿含有的資料、由海關通報的資料與其他相關的資料來源，包括依據第15條第2項與第25條規定進行監督與檢查。

執委會亦應促進與主管機關關於詐欺活動的資訊交流與依據第26條規定科處罰金。

4. 在經核准CBAM申報人未依據第6條提出CBAM申報時、或在基於本條第2項規定的審查，執委會認為所申報的CBAM憑證號碼不正確時，執委會應依據其所掌握的資料評估該經核准CBAM申報人的義務。執委會應建立一個應繳交CBAM憑證總數的初步計算，最遲應在提出CBAM申報次年的12月31日前或最遲在不正確CBAM申報提出後第四年的12月31日前，適用初步計算。執委會應提供給主管機關這個初步計算，僅供參考，並不影響經核准CBAM申報人設立所在會員國主管機關確定的最終計算。

5. 在主管機關得出結論，應繳交的CBAM憑證所申報的數目不正確時、或未依據第6條提出CBAM申報時，考量執委會提出的資料，主管機關應確定經核准CBAM申報人應繳交CBAM憑證的數目。

主管機關應通知經核准CBAM申報人其所確定CBAM憑證數目的決定，並應要求該經核准CBAM申報人在一個月內應繳交CBAM憑證。

主管機關的決定應含有作成決定的理由與關於申訴權的資訊。透過CBAM登記簿，決定亦應通知執委會。

在收到執委會依據本條第2項與第4項規定的初步計算後，主管機關決定不採取任何行動時，透過CBAM登記簿，從而主管機關應告知執委會。

6. 在主管機關得出結論，所繳交的CBAM憑證數目超過應繳交的數目時，主管機關應立即告知執委會。應依據第23條規定買回超過所繳交的CBAM憑證。

第四章

CBAM憑證

第20條 │ CBAM憑證之出售

1. 會員國應在共同的中央平台出售CBAM憑證給設立於該會員國經核准CBAM申報人。

2. 執委會應設立與管理共同的中央平台，遵循在執委會與會員國間的聯合採購程序。

   執委會與主管機關應可進用在共同中央平台的資料。

3. 在每個工作日結束時，應移轉在共同中央平台關於出售、買回與註銷CBAM憑證的資料給CBAM登記簿。

4. CBAM憑證應以第21條規定計算的價格賣給經核准CBAM申報人。

5. 執委會應確保每個CBAM憑證核發時有一個獨有的辨

識號碼。執委會應在CBAM登記簿的經核准CBAM申報人帳戶購買憑證時，登記此一獨有的辨識號碼、價格與CBAM的購買日期。

6. 依據第28條規定，執委會應公布授權法補充本規章，以更進一步具體規定出售及買回CBAM憑證的時程、行政程序與其他關於管理的事項、尋求與2010年第1031號執委會規章的程序進行整合。

第21條｜CBAM憑證的價格

1. 執委會應依據2010年第1031號規章規定的程序，對每個日曆週，以在歐盟ETS配額拍賣平台收盤的平均價格計算出CBAM憑證的價格。

   對於在拍賣平台無拍賣日期的日曆週，CBAM憑證的價格應為在拍賣平台進行拍賣最後一週歐盟ETS配額收盤的平均價格。

2. 針對第1項第2段規定，執委會應在其網頁或以任何其他適當的方式在下一個日曆週的第一個工作日公告平均價格。

3. 授權執委會公布適用本條第1項規定的方法，以計算CBAM憑證的平均價格，並公告該價格的實際運作。應依據第29條第2項規定的檢驗程序，公布這些施行法。

第22條 | 繳交CBAM憑證

1. 在每年5月31日前，與在2027年首次對2026年，核准CBAM申報人應透過CBAM登記簿繳交相當於依據第6條第2項第c款規定申報及依據第8條規定經認證的內含排放量前一個日曆年的CBAM憑證數目。執委會應從CBAM登記簿移除已繳交的CBAM憑證。經核准CBAM申報人應確保在其CBAM登記簿帳戶有所需的CBAM憑證數目。

2. 經核准CBAM申報人應確保在每個季度結束時，在其CBAM登記簿帳戶的CBAM憑證數目相當於自日曆年開始所有進口產品以依據附件四規定公式計算的默認值確定內含排放量至少80%。

3. 在執委會發現在經核准CBAM申報人帳戶內的CBAM憑證數目不符合第2項規定的義務時，透過CBAM登記簿，執委會應告知經核准CBAM申報人設立所在會員國的主管機關。

   主管機關應通知經核准CBAM申報人應確保在此一通知的一個月內在其帳戶內有足夠的CBAM憑證數目。

   主管機關應在CBAM登記簿登記通知經核准CBAM申報人與自經核准CBAM申報人的回應。

第23條 | 買回CBAM憑證

1. 在依據第22條繳交憑證後，經核准CBAM申報人請求

在核准CBAM申報人設立所在會員國應買回在CBAM登記簿申報人多餘的CBAM憑證。

透過第20條規定的共同中央平台為經核准CBAM申報人設立所在會員國的利益，執委會應買回多餘的CBAM憑證。在每年6月31日以前，在繳交CBAM憑證的期間，經核准CBAM申報人應提出買回請求。

2. 第1項規定買回憑證的數目僅限於在前一個日曆年間由經核准CBAM申報人所購買CBAM憑證總數的三分之一。

3. 每個憑證買回的價格應為經核准CBAM申報人在購買該憑證時所支付的價格。

第24條｜註銷CBAM憑證

每年7月1日，執委會應註銷在前一個日曆年度以前的一年間購買而仍在CBAM登記簿內經核准CBAM申報人帳戶的CBAM憑證。無任何賠償應註銷這些CBAM憑證。

應繳交CBAM憑證數目有爭議繫屬於會員國的爭訟時，執委會應就有爭議的數量中止CBAM的註銷。核准CBAM申報人設立的會員國主管機關應立即告知執委會所有相關的資訊。

適用於產品進口的規則

第25條｜適用於產品進口的規則

1. 海關不應允許由非經核准CBAM申報人的其他人進口產品。

2. 海關應定期且自動，特別是以依據2013年第952號規章第56條第5項規定建立的監督機制，通知執委會申報進口產品的具體資料。該資料應包括EORI號碼與經核准CBAM申報人的CBAM帳號、產品的CN 8位碼、數量、原產國、報關日期與海關程序。

3. 執委會應通知經核准CBAM申報人設立所在會員國的主管機關於本條第2項規定的資料，並應對每個CBAM申報人與第14條規定登記簿的資料交叉檢查比對該資料。

4. 依據2013年第952號規章第12條第1項規定，海關得告知執委會與給予核准CBAM申報人身份的會員國主管機關於由海關在執行職務時取得的機密資料或在機密的基礎上，提供給海關的機密資料。

5. 1997年第515號規章應準用於本規章。

6. 授權執委會公布施行法，定義資料的範圍與週期性、本條第2項規定資料的通知時間與方法。應依據第29條第2項規定的檢驗程序，公布這些施行法。

施行

第26條│罰金

1. 在每年5月31日前，經核准CBAM申報人未繳交相當於自前一個日曆年在進口產品的內含排放量，應負責任支付罰金。此一罰金應完全相等於2003年第87號指令第16條第3項規定的超過排放罰金，並依據該指令第16條第4項規定提高罰金，適用於產品進口的年度。此一罰金亦適用於經核准CBAM申報人未繳交的每個CBAM憑證。

2. 不同於經核准CBAM申報人的其他人，引進產品到歐盟關稅領域而未遵循本規章的義務時，這個人應負責任支付罰金。這個罰金應有效、適當、及具勸阻作用，特別是取決於此一未遵循的持續時間、嚴重程度、範圍、故意的性質與重複、以及這個人配合主管機關的程度，金額從第1項規定罰金三倍至五倍，對這個人未繳交的每個CBAM憑證，適用引進產品的年度。

3. 罰金的支付不應免除經核准CBAM申報人繳交在具體年度未交CBAM憑證數目的義務。

4. 若主管機關決定，包括依據第19條規定由執委會所做的初步計算在內，經核准CBAM申報人未遵循本條第1項規定繳交CBAM憑證、或引進產品到歐盟關稅領域

的人未遵循規定於本條第2項的本規章義務時，主管機關應依據本條第1項或第2項規定科處罰金。為此一目的，主管機關應通知經核准CBAM申報人，或在適用本條第2項時，這個人：

(a) 主管機關得出結論，經核准CBAM申報人或本條第2項規定的人未遵循本規章的義務；

(b) 其結論的理由；

(c) 對經核准CBAM申報人或本條第2項規定的人科處罰金的金額；

(d) 罰金到期之日期；

(e) 經核准CBAM申報人或本條第2項規定的人應採取行動支付罰金；與

(f) 經核准CBAM申報人或本條第2項規定的人之申訴權。

5. 在第4項第d款規定到期前未支付罰金時，主管機關應盡其所能以相關會員國的國內法保障支付該罰金。

6. 會員國應告知執委會第1項及第2項規定的罰金決定，並應在CBAM登記簿登記第5項規定的最終支付。

第27條│規避

1. 依據本條規定，基於相關與客觀的資料，執委會應採取行動解決規避本規章的做法。

2. 規避做法的定義為產品貿易模式的變化，其源於實

踐、過程或工作，除完全或部分避免本規章規定的任何義務外，無充分的正當理由或經濟理由。此一實踐、過程或工作得包含，但不限於：

(a) 對相關產品進行輕微變更，使這些產品屬於附件一清單未表列的CN號碼，但變更改變了其基本特性，不在此限。

(b) 人為的分裝運送產品，其內在價值不超過第2條第3項規定的門檻值。

3. 針對辨識規避做法，包括透過市場監督或基於任何相關的資料來源，例如由民間組織提出與所報告的資料，執委會應持續監督歐盟層級的情況。

4. 受第2項規定任何情況影響或受益的一會員國或任何的當事人，若面對規避做法時，得通知執委會。不同於直接受影響或受益當事人的其他利益團體，例如環保組織與非政府組織，發現規避做法正確的證據時，並得通知執委會。

5. 第4項規定的通知應陳述所根據的理由，且應包括相關的資料與支持主張本規章的規避統計資料。由一個會員國通知、或由一個受影響、受益或其他利益當事人通知，而通知符合本項的要件時、或執委會本身決定有必要進行一個調查時，執委會應啟動一個規避主張的調查。在進行調查時，執委會得由主管機關與海關協助。在自通知日起九個月內，執委會應完成調查。

在啟動調查後，執委會應通知所有主管機關。

6. 考慮相關資料、報告與統計資料，包括由海關提供的資料在內，執委會有充分理由相信本條第2項第a款規定的規避以既定模式正發生於一個或數個會員國時，應依據第28條規定授權執委會公布授權法，為反規避的目的，以增加本條第2項第a款相關輕微變更的產品，修訂附件一清單表列產品。

第七章

授權之執行與委員會程序

第28條｜授權之執行

1. 授權執委會公布授權法，應遵守本條規定的條件。

2. 自2023年5月17日起五年期限內，應授權執委會公布第2條第10項、第2條第11項、第18條第3項、第20條第6項與第27條第6項規定的授權法。在五年期限結束前不遲於九個月，針對授權，執委會應做成一個報告。應默認延長授權到相同期間的期限，但在每個期限結束前不遲於三個月，歐洲議會或理事會反對此一延長時，不在此限。

3. 隨時得由歐洲議會或理事會撤回第2條第10項、第2條第11項、第18條第3項、第20條第6項與第27條第6項規定的授權。

4. 撤回決定應在決定中，具體規定授權的結束。應在歐盟官方公報公告決定次日或具體規定之後的一個日期生效。不應影響任何已經生效授權法的效力。

5. 在公布授權法以前，依據2016年4月13日機關間最佳立法協議規定的原則，執委會應諮詢由每個會員國指定的專家。

6. 只要公布了授權法，執委會應同時通知歐洲議會與理事會。

7. 僅在歐洲議會或理事會在該授權法通知歐洲議會與理事會二個月期限內明確表示不反對時、或在該期限屆滿前，歐洲議會與理事會均告知執委會都不反對時，第2條第10項、第2條第11項、第18條第3項、第20條第6項與第27條第6項規定的授權法應生效。依據歐洲議會或理事會的提議，該期限應延期二個月。

第29條｜委員會程序

1. 應由CBAM委員會協助執委會。CBAM委員會應為2011年第182號規章意義的委員會。

2. 針對本項的參考，應適用2011年第182號規章第5條規定。

報告與審查

第30條｜執委會的審查與報告

1. 諮商相關的利害關係人後，針對擴大本規章適用範圍所指稱及第2項第a款規定與發展根據環境足跡方法計算內含排放量方法，執委會應收集所需的資料。

2. 在第32條規定的過渡時期結束前，執委會應向歐洲議會與理事會提出一份關於適用本規章的報告。

   報告應含有評估下列的事項：

   (a) 擴大適用範圍到下列事項的可能性：

      (i) 在附件二清單表列產品內含間接排放量；

      (ii) 在附件一清單表列產品的運輸與運輸服務的內含排放量；

      (iii) 不同於附件一清單表列產品，有碳洩漏風險的產品與特別是有機化學品及聚合物；

      (iv) 對附件一清單表列產品的其他投入材料（前體）；

   (b) 基於2003年第87號指令第10b條規定辨別有碳洩漏風險產業部門，使用於辨別本規章附件一清單所包含產品的標準；該評估應附具一份結束於2030年的時間表逐步納入在本規章適用範圍內的產品，特別考慮其個別碳洩漏風險程度；

(c) 對納入附件一清單表列的其他產品，計算內含排放量的技術要件；

(d) 針對氣候行動在國際討論所做的進展；

(e) 治理制度，包括行政費用在內；

(f) 本規章對來自依據聯合國認定為最低度開發國家有特別利益的開發中國家進口附件一清單表列產品與給予技術協助效果的衝擊；

(g) 依據第7條第7項與附件四第4.3點規定間接排放量的計算方法。

3. 至少在過渡時期結束前一年，執委會應向歐洲議會與理事會提出一份報告，辨別在附件一清單表列產品下游價值鏈產品認為應納入本規章適用範圍的建議。為達成此一目的，執委會應及時發展一個基於累積（加總）溫室氣體排放與碳洩漏風險用語的方法。

4. 第2項與第3項規定的報告，在適當時，在過渡時期結束前，應附具一份法案，包括詳細的衝擊評估，特別是針對基於在報告的推論擴大本規章的適用範圍。

5. 自過渡時期結束起每二年，作為給歐洲議會與理事會關於2003年第87號指令第10條第5項規定年度報告的一部分，以說明為了出口到不適用歐盟ETS或類似碳定價機制的第三國，執委會應評估CBAM的效益。報告應特別評估在CBAM產業部門歐盟出口的發展與關於這些產品在全球市場的貿易流量及內含排放量的發展。

歐盟CBAM法規：台灣廠商因應之道與申報準備

在報告做成結論為出口到不適用歐盟ETS或類似碳定價機制的第三國，在歐盟境內生產的產品存在碳洩漏風險時，在適當時，執委會應提出法案，指明風險遵循WTO法規與考慮在歐盟設施的脫碳。

6. 針對評價衝擊與適用可能的調整，執委會應監督CBAM發揮的作用。

在2028年1月1日前、以及之後每二年，執委會應向歐洲議會與理事會提出一份適用本規章與CBAM發揮作用的報告。報告至少應含有下列的事項：

(a) 評估對下列事項的CBAM衝擊：

   (i) 碳洩漏，包括相關的出口；

   (ii) 涵蓋的產業部門；

   (iii) 內部市場、在全部歐盟的經濟及領域衝擊；

   (iv) 商品的通貨膨脹與價格；

   (v) 對使用附件一清單表列產品工業的影響；

   (vi) 國際貿易，包括資源洗牌；與

   (vii) 最低度發展的國家；

(b) 評估：

   (i) 治理制度，包括由會員國施行與管理核准CBAM申報人；

   (ii) 本規章的適用範圍；

   (iii) 規避做法；

   (iv) 適用會員國的罰金；

(c) 調查的結果與所科處罰金；

(d) 在附件一清單表列不同產品每個原產國排放強度的加總資料。

7. 在應遵守CBAM的一個或數個第三國發生了無法掌控的無法預見、例外與無緣無故的事件，且該事件對這些相關國家的經濟及工業基礎設施造成破壞性後果時，執委會應評估情況與向歐洲議會和理事會提出報告，適當時並附具法案，以修訂本規章規定必要的暫時措施解決這些例外的情況。

8. 自本規章第32條規定的過渡時期結束時起，作為依據2021年第947號第41條規定年度報告的一部分，執委會應評價與報告在該規章的經費提供如何分配給在最低度開發國家的製造業脫碳技術。

與歐盟ETS的免費配額協調

第31條｜歐盟ETS的免費配額與CBAM憑證的繳交義務

1. 為反映2003年第87號指令第10a條規定的歐盟ETS免費配額分配，按本規章附件一清單表列在歐盟內設施的生產，應調整本規章應繳交的CBAM憑證。

2. 授權執委會公布施行法，詳細規定本規章第1項規定的調整計算規則。這些詳細的規則應參考適用在附件一

清單表列產品在歐盟境內設施生產的歐盟ETS免費配額原則、考慮針對結合這些標竿直到相關產品的相應值與考慮相關投入材料（前體），加以規定。應依據本規章第29條第2項規定的檢驗程序，公布這些施行法。

過渡時期

第32條 | 過渡時期的範圍

自2023年10月1日至2025年12月31日的過渡時期，本規章進口商品的義務應限於規定在本規章第33條、第34條與第35條的申報義務。設立於一會員國的進口商與依據2013年第952號規章第18條規定指定一位間接海關代表人，而間接海關代表人同意，申報義務適用於該間接海關代表人。在非設立於一會員國進口商的情形，申報義務應適用於間接海關代表人。

第33條 | 產品的進口

1. 不遲於放行商品自由流通時，海關應告知進口商或32條情形的間接海關代表人關於第35條的申報義務。

2. 海關應定期及自動，特別是以2013年第952號共同關稅法規章第56條第5項規定建立的監督機制或以電子資料傳輸方法，告知執委會關於進口產品的資料，包括由

歐盟境外加工程序的加工品在內。這些資料包括海關申報人與進口商的EORI號碼、8位的CN碼、數量、原產國、海關申報日期與通關程序。

3. 執委會應告知海關申報人與進口商設立所在會員國的主管機關第2項的資料。

第34條 │ 特定關務程序的申報義務

1. 進口2013年第952號共同關稅法規章第256條規定在歐盟境內加工程序的加工產品時，第35條的申報義務應包括關於產品在境內進行加工程序地點與產生進口的加工產品的資料，即便加工產品非本規章附件一的清單產品。本項亦適用於在歐盟境內進行加工程序加工產品在2013年第952號共同關稅法規章第205條規定的退貨情形。

2. 第35條的申報義務不適用於下列的進口：

   (a) 2013年第952號共同關稅法規章第259條規定在歐盟境外進行加工程序所生產的加工產品；

   (b) 構成2013年第952號共同關稅法規章第205條規定退貨的產品。

第35條 │ 申報義務

1. 在日曆年的特定季度進口產品時，第32條規定的進口商、間接海關代表人應對該季度繳交CBAM報告。

CBAM報告應包含在該季度的進口產品資料，不遲於該季度結束後一個月繳交給執委會。

2. CBAM報告應包含下列的資料：

(a) 以兆瓦時說明電力及以噸說明其他產品、按每個設施在原產國生產的產品類型，表述每個類型產品的總量；

(b) 以每兆瓦時電力產生的碳排放噸數及以每種產品類型每噸排放的碳排放噸數說明其他產品、依據附件四的計算方法說明實際內含排放的總量；

(c) 依據施行法計算第7項的總間接排放量；

(d) 在進口產品內含排放量已經在原產國繳交的碳費，考慮所有的扣減或其他形式的補償。

3. 執委會應定期通知相關的主管機關這些進口商的清單或設立於會員國的間接海關代表人清單，包括有正當理由認為未履行第1項規定繳交CBAM報告的義務。

4. 執委會認為CBAM報告不完全或不正確時，應通知進口商設立所在會員國的主管機關或第32條規定的情形，間接海關代表人所在會員國的主管機關，應繳交完全或更正報告所需的額外資料。主管機關應啟動更正程序，並通知進口商或第32條規定的情形，間接海關代表人應繳交更正報告所需的額外資料。在適當時，進口商或間接海關代表人應繳交一份更正報告給相關的主管機關與執委會。

5. 會員國主管機關啟動本條第4項規定的更正程序，包括收到第4項規定的相關資料在內，與決定進口商或第32條規定的情形，間接海關代表人未採取必要步驟更正CBAM報告，或相關的主管機關決定，包括考量第3項規定收到資料在內，進口商或第32條規定的情形，間接海關代表人未履行第1項規定繳交CBAM報告時，該主管機關應科處進口商或第32條規定的情形，間接海關代表人有效、適當與有勸阻作用的罰金。為此，主管機關應通知進口商或第32條規定的情形，間接海關代表人，並告知執委會下列的事項：

    (a) 結論與結論的理由、進口商或第32條規定的情形，間接海關代表人未履行繳交季度的CBAM報告或採取必要的步驟更正報告；

    (b) 科處進口商或第32條規定的情形，間接海關代表人的罰金金額；

    (c) 罰金自何時生效的日期；

    (d) 進口商或第32條規定的情形，間接海關代表人應採取行動支付罰金；與

    (e) 進口商或第32條規定的情形，間接海關代表人申訴的權利。

6. 在從執委會收到本條規定的資料後，主管機關決定不採取行動時，主管機關應告知執委會。

7. 授權執委會通過關於下列事務的施行法：

(a) 應申報的資料、申報的方法與表格，包括按原產國與產品類型的詳細資料，以支持第2項第a款、第b款與第c款的總量、以及第2項第d款規定任何相關扣減或其他形式補償的例子；

(b) 依據第5項規定應科處罰金的指示範圍與考量決定實際金額的標準，包括不履行報告的嚴重程度與持續的期間。

(c) 關於第2項第d款規定的平均碳費按平均匯率換算為外幣的詳細規則；

(d) 附件四規定計算方法要素的詳細規則，包括決定生產程序的系統界限、排放係數、設施實際排放的特定值與其分別應用個別產品的特定值、以及規定方法確保數據的可信賴，包括詳細的程度；

(e) 在進口產品間接排放申報要件的方法與表格；表格應包括附件一清單表列產品生產時所使用電量、原產國、發電來源與關於該電力的排放係數。

應依據本規章第29條第2項規定的檢驗程序（examination procedure），公布這些施行法。這些施行法應適用本規章第32條規定的過渡時期內進口產品，並在現有的法律基礎上，適用2003年第87號ETS指令的設施。

最終條款

第36條｜生效

1. 本規章應自公告於歐盟官方公報次日起生效。

2. 自2023年10月1日起適用，但

    (a) 自2024年12月31日起，應適用第5條、第10條、第14條、第16條與第17條。

    (b) 自2026年1月1日起，應適用第2條第2項、第4條、第6條至第9條、第15條與第19條、第20條第1項、第3項、第4項及第5項、第21條至第27條與第31條。

本規章全部應具有拘束力與直接適用於全體會員國。

於史特拉斯堡，2023年5月10日

依據進口貨品稅則稅號表列
適用CBAM的產品清單

水泥

CN code	溫室氣體
CN 2507 00 80 －其他高嶺土質黏土	二氧化碳
CN 2523 10 00 －白色水泥	二氧化碳
CN 2523 21 00 －白水泥，不論是否人工著色	二氧化碳
CN 2523 29 00 －其他Portland水泥	二氧化碳
CN 2523 30 00 －鋁質水泥	二氧化碳
CN 2523 90 00 －其他水硬性水泥	二氧化碳

電力

CN code	溫室氣體
CN 2716 00 00 －電力	二氧化碳

肥料

CN code	溫室氣體
CN 2808 00 00 －硝酸、磺硝酸	二氧化碳與一氧化氮
CN 2814 －無水氨或氨水溶液	二氧化碳
CN 2834 21 00 －鉀之硝酸鹽	二氧化碳與一氧化氮
CN 3102 －礦物或化學氮肥	二氧化碳與一氧化氮
CN3105 －礦物或化學肥料內含有肥料三要素氮、磷、鉀中之兩種或三種者；其他化學肥料；本章所載貨品之屬錠劑或類似形狀者，或其包裝毛重不超過10公斤者——但不包括3105 60 00 －礦物或化學肥料要素磷及鉀者	二氧化碳與一氧化氮

鋼與鐵

CN code	溫室氣體
CN 72 －鋼與鐵 但不包括： 7202 2 －合金鐵 7202 30 00 －矽錳鐵 7202 50 00 －矽鉻鐵 7202 70 00 －鉬鐵 7202 8000 －鎢鐵及矽鎢鐵 7202 91 00 －鈦鐵及矽鈦鐵 7202 92 00 －釩鐵 7202 93 00 －鈮鐵 7202 99 －其他： 7202 99 10 －磷鐵 7202 99 30 －矽鎂鐵 7202 99 80 －其他 7204 －鐵屬廢料及碎屑；重熔用廢鋼鑄錠	二氧化碳
CN 2601 12 00 －已凝聚之鐵礦石及其精砂，已焙燒之硫化鐵礦石除外	二氧化碳
CN 7301 －不論已否鑽孔、衝孔或以元件組成之鋼板樁；經焊接之鋼鐵角、形及型	二氧化碳
CN 7302 －鐵道及電車道建軌鋼鐵材料：軌、護軌、齒軌、道岔尖軌、轍叉、尖軌拉桿及其他叉道段件、枕鐵、軌枕、魚尾板、軌座、軌座楔、底板、軌夾、座板、繫桿及其他連接或固定鐵軌之專用材料	二氧化碳
CN 7303 00 －鑄鐵製管及空心型	二氧化碳
CN 7304 －鋼鐵製（鑄鐵除外）無縫管及空心型油、氣管線用管	二氧化碳
CN 7305 －其他鋼鐵管（如焊接、鉚接或類似接合者），具圓橫斷面，其外徑超過406.4公釐的油、氣管線用管。	二氧化碳
CN 7306 －鋼鐵製之其他管及空心型（如開縫或焊接、鉚接或類似接合者）油、氣管線用管	二氧化碳
CN 7307 －鋼鐵製管之配件（如接頭、肘管、套筒）鑄造配件	二氧化碳

歐盟CBAM法規：台灣廠商因應之道與申報準備

CN code	溫室氣體
CN 7308 －鋼鐵結構物（第9406節組合建築物除外）及其零件（如橋及橋體段、水閘、塔、格狀桅桿、屋頂、屋頂假、門窗及其框架及門檻、百葉窗、欄杆、柱）；鋼鐵製板、桿、角形、型、管及類似品，已製作備結構物用者	二氧化碳
CN 7309 00 －貯藏任何材料（壓縮或液化氣體除外）用之鋼鐵製貯器、容槽、大桶及類似容器，其容量超過300公升，不論是否經襯裏或隔熱，但無機械或熱力設備者	二氧化碳
CN 7310 －貯藏任何材料（壓縮或液化氣體除外）用之鋼鐵製貯器、容槽、大桶及類似容器，其容量超過300公升，不論是否經襯裏或隔熱，但無機械或熱力設備者	二氧化碳
CN 7311 00 －供貯存壓縮或液化氣體用之鋼鐵製容器	二氧化碳
CN 7318 －鋼鐵製螺釘、螺栓、螺帽、車用螺釘、螺旋鉤、鉚釘、橫梢、開口梢、墊圈（包括彈簧墊圈）及類似製品	二氧化碳
CN 7326 －其他鋼鐵製品	二氧化碳

鋁

CN code	溫室氣體
CN 7601 －未經塑性加工鋁	二氧化碳與全氟碳化合物
CN 7603 －鋁粉及鱗片	二氧化碳與全氟碳化合物
CN 7604 －鋁條、桿及型材	二氧化碳與全氟碳化合物
CN 7605 －鋁線	二氧化碳與全氟碳化合物
CN 7606 －鋁板、片及扁條，厚度超過0.2公厘者	二氧化碳與全氟碳化合物
CN 7607 －鋁箔（不論是否印花或以紙、紙板、塑膠或類似襯墊者），其厚度（不包括襯物）不超過0.2公釐者	二氧化碳與全氟碳化合物

CN code	溫室氣體
CN 7608－鋁管	二氧化碳與全氟碳化合物
CN 7609 0000－鋁製管配件（如接頭、肘管、套管）	二氧化碳與全氟碳化合物
CN 7610－鋁製結構物（第9406節之組合式建築物除外）及其零件（例如：橋及橋體段、塔、格狀桅桿、屋頂、屋頂架、門、窗、及其框架及門檻、欄杆、柱）；鋁板、桿、型材、管及類似品，已製作備結構物用者	二氧化碳與全氟碳化合物
CN 7611 0000－鋁製貯器、容槽、桶及類似容器供貯存任何材料（不包括壓縮或液化氣），其容量超過300公升，不論是否經襯裏或隔熱，但無機械或熱力設備者	二氧化碳與全氟碳化合物
CN 7612－鋁製箱、桶、罐、盒、及類似容器（包括堅固或可壓扁之管狀容器），供盛裝任何材料（不包括壓縮或液化氣）用者，其容量不超過300公升，不論是否經襯裏或隔熱，但無機械或熱力設備者	二氧化碳與全氟碳化合物
CN 7613 0000－供貯存壓縮或液化氣體用之鋁製容器	二氧化碳與全氟碳化合物
CN 7614－鋁製絞股線、纜、編帶及類似品，非電絕緣者	二氧化碳與全氟碳化合物
CN 7616－其他鋁製品	二氧化碳與全氟碳化合物

化學產品

CN code	溫室氣體
CN2804 10000－氫	二氧化碳

歐盟CBAM法規：台灣廠商因應之道與申報準備

依據第7條第1項規定，僅應考慮直接排放量的產品清單

鋼與鐵

CN code	溫室氣體
CN 72 －鋼與鐵 —— 但不包括： —— 7202 2 －合金鐵 —— 7202 30 00 －矽錳鐵 —— 7202 50 00 －矽鉻鐵 —— 7202 70 00 －鉬鐵 —— 7202 80 00 －鎢鐵及矽鎢鐵 —— 7202 91 00 －鈦鐵及矽鈦鐵 —— 7202 92 00 －釩鐵 —— 7202 93 00 －鈮鐵 —— 7202 99 －其他 —— 7202 99 10 －磷鐵 —— 7202 99 30 －矽鎂鐵 —— 7202 99 80 －其他 —— 7204 －鐵屬廢料及碎屑；重熔用廢鋼鑄錠。	二氧化碳
CN 7301 －不論已否鑽孔、衝孔或以元件組成之鋼板樁；經焊接之鋼鐵角、形及型	二氧化碳
CN 7302 －鐵道及電車道建軌鋼鐵材料：軌、護軌、齒軌、道岔尖軌、轍叉、尖軌拉桿及其他叉道段件、枕鐵、軌枕、魚尾板、軌座、軌座楔、底板、軌夾、座板、繫桿及其他連接或固定鐵軌之專用材料	二氧化碳
CN 7303 00 －鑄鐵製管及空心型	二氧化碳
CN 7304 －鋼鐵製（鑄鐵除外）無縫管及空心型油、氣管線用管	二氧化碳
CN 7305 －其他鋼鐵管（如焊接、鉚接或類似接合者），具圓橫斷面，其外徑超過406.4公釐的油、氣管線用管	二氧化碳

CN code	溫室氣體
CN 7306 －鋼鐵製之其他管及空心型（如開縫或焊接、鉚接或類似接合者）油、氣管線用管	二氧化碳
CN 7307 －鋼鐵製管之配件（如接頭、肘管、套筒）鑄造配件	二氧化碳
CN 7308 －鋼鐵結構物（第9406節組合建築物除外）及其零件（如橋及橋體段、水閘、塔、格狀桅桿、屋頂、屋頂假、門窗及其框架及門檻、百葉窗、欄杆、柱）；鋼鐵製板、桿、角形、型、管及類似品，已製作備結構物用者	二氧化碳
CN 7309 00 －貯藏任何材料（壓縮或液化氣體除外）用之鋼鐵製貯器、容槽、大桶及類似容器，其容量超過300公升，不論是否經襯裏或隔熱，但無機械或熱力設備者	二氧化碳
CN 7310 －貯藏任何材料（壓縮或液化氣體除外）用之鋼鐵製貯器、容槽、大桶及類似容器，其容量超過300公升，不論是否經襯裏或隔熱，但無機械或熱力設備者	二氧化碳
CN 7311 00 －供貯存壓縮或液化氣體用之鋼鐵製容器	二氧化碳
CN 7318 －鋼鐵製螺釘、螺栓、螺帽、車用螺釘、螺旋鉤、鉚釘、橫梢、開口梢、墊圈（包括彈簧墊圈）及類似製品	二氧化碳
CN 7326 －其他鋼鐵製品	二氧化碳

鋁

CN code	溫室氣體
CN 7601 －未經塑性加工鋁	二氧化碳與全氟碳化合物
CN 7603 －鋁粉及鱗片	二氧化碳與全氟碳化合物
CN 7604 －鋁條、桿及型材	二氧化碳與全氟碳化合物
CN 7605 －鋁線	二氧化碳與全氟碳化合物
CN 7606 －鋁板、片及扁條，厚度超過0.2公釐者	二氧化碳與全氟碳化合物

CN code	溫室氣體
CN 7607－鋁箔（不論是否印花或以紙、紙板、塑膠或類似襯墊者），其厚度（不包括襯物）不超過0.2公釐者	二氧化碳與全氟碳化合物
CN 7608－鋁管	二氧化碳與全氟碳化合物
CN 7609 0000－鋁製管配件（如接頭、肘管、套管）	二氧化碳與全氟碳化合物
CN 7610－鋁製結構物（第9406節之組合式建築物除外）及其零件（例如：橋及橋體段、塔、格狀桅桿、屋頂、屋頂架、門、窗、及其框架及門檻、欄杆、柱）；鋁板、桿、型材、管及類似品，已製作備結構物用者	二氧化碳與全氟碳化合物
CN 7611 0000－鋁製貯器、容槽、桶及類似容器供貯存任何材料（不包括壓縮或液化氣），其容量超過300公升，不論是否經襯裏或隔熱，但無機械或熱力設備者	二氧化碳與全氟碳化合物
CN 7612－鋁製箱、桶、罐、盒、及類似容器（包括堅固或可壓扁之管狀容器），供盛裝任何材料（不包括壓縮或液化氣）用者，其容量不超過300公升，不論是否經襯裏或隔熱，但無機械或熱力設備者	二氧化碳與全氟碳化合物
CN 7613 0000－供貯存壓縮或液化氣體用之鋁製容器	二氧化碳與全氟碳化合物
CN 7614－鋁製絞股線、纜、編帶及類似品，非電絕緣者	二氧化碳與全氟碳化合物
CN 7616－其他鋁製品	二氧化碳與全氟碳化合物

化學產品

CN code	溫室氣體
CN 2804 10000－氫	二氧化碳

為第2條之目的，
本規章範圍外的第三國與領域

1. 本規章範圍外的第三國與領域

本規章不應適用於來自下列國家的產品：

— 冰島

— 列支敦斯登

— 挪威

— 瑞士

本規章不應適用於來自下列領域的產品：

— 布辛根（Büsingen）

— 黑爾戈蘭（Heligoland）

— 利維尼奧（Livigno）

— 休達（Ceuta）

— 美利亞（Melilla）

2. 本規章範圍外的第三國與領域針對電力進口至歐盟關稅領域

（依據第2條第11項規定，由執委會增加或移除第三國或領域）

依據第7條規定，內含排放量的計算方法

1. 定義

為本附件、附件五與附件六之目的，適用下列的定義：

(a) 簡單產品係指在生產過程中生產的產品僅需要零內含排放的投入材料（前體）和燃料；

(b) 複雜產品係指非簡單產品的其他產品；

(c) 具體的內含排放係指一噸產品的內含排放量，以每噸產品的二氧化碳排放噸數（CO_2e）表示；

(d) 二氧化碳排放係數係指在一個地理區域內，自化石燃料發電的二氧化碳強度的加權平均值；二氧化碳排放係數是電力部門的二氧化碳排放數據除以基於化石燃料在相關的地理區域的總發電的結果；它以每兆瓦時二氧化碳的噸數表示；

(e) 「電力排放係數」係指默認值，以CO_2e表示，意謂在生產產品消耗電力的排放強度；

(f) 購電協議係指一個人同意直接從電力生產商購買電力的契約；

(g) 「輸電系統營運商」係指2019年第944號指令第2條第35項定義的營運商。

2. 確定簡單產品的實際具體內含排放量

為確定具體設施生產的簡單產品的具體實際內含排放量，應計算直接排放量與在適用間接排放量的情況。為此目的，應適用下列的公式：

$$SEE_g = \frac{AttrEm_g}{AL_g}$$

SEE_g是產品g具體的內含排放量，以每噸CO_2e表示；

$AttrEm_g$係指歸因於產品g的排放；與

AL_g是產品g在申報期間在生產產品的設施的產品數量。

「歸因排放」係指申報期間設施排放的一部分，係在適用依據第7條第7項公布的施行法所定義的生產過程系統界限時，由生產產品g的生產過程所產生的排放。應依據下列的公式計算歸因排放：

$$AttrEm_g = DirEm + IndirEm$$

$DirEm$是直接排放，在依據第7條第7項公布的施行法所規定系統界限內，生產過程中產生的排放，以CO_2e噸數表示；與

$IndirEm$是在依據第7條第7項公布的施行法所規定系統界限內，由在產品生產過程消耗電力的電力生產產生的間接排放，以CO_2e噸數表示。

歐盟CBAM法規：台灣廠商因應之道與申報準備

3. 確定複雜產品的實際內含排放量

為確定具體設施生產的複雜產品的具體實際內含排放量，應適用下列的公式：

$$SEE_g = \frac{At\ tr\ Em_g + EE_{InpMat}}{AL_g}$$

AttrEmg係指歸因於產品g的排放；

ALg是產品g在申報期間在該設施生產的產品總量；與

EEinpMat是生產過程中所消耗投入材料（前體）的內含排放量。僅以在依據第7條第7項公布的施行法列示與生產過程的系統界限相關的投入材料（前體）。相關的EEinpMat計算如下：

$$EE_{InpMat} = \sum_{i=1}^{n} M_i \cdot SEE_i$$

Mi是生產過程中所使用投入材料（前體）i的數量，

SEEi是投入材料（前體）i的具體內含排放量。對於SEEi，設施營運商應使用生產投入材料的設施所產生的排放量，且可以充分測量該設施的數據。

4. 確定第7條第2項與第3項規定的默認值

為確定默認值之目的，應僅使用實際排放量，確定內含排放量。在無實際資料時，得使用文獻值。在收集確定附件一清單表列產品每個類型相關默認值所需的數據前，執委會應公布

生產過程投入的廢氣或溫室氣體的更正方法指南。應依據最佳可用數據確定默認值。最佳可用數據應基於可靠和公開可取得的資料。透過第7條第7項規定的施行法依據最新和可靠的資訊，包括依據第三國或第三國群組提供的資料，應定期修訂默認值。

4.1. 第7條第2項規定的默認值

若經核准的CBAM申報人無法適當確定實際排放量時，應使用默認值。這些默認值應按每個與附件一清單表列每個產品的平均排放強度，以及對電力以外，以適當設計的增加加價。加價幅度應依據第7條第7項公布的施行法確定，且應在適當的程度規定加價幅度，以確保CBAM的環境完整性、以最新及可靠的資料為基礎，包括在過渡時期收集到的資料在內。若對出口國可靠的資料無法適用於產品的一個類型時，默認值應依據在適用歐盟ETS該產品類型表現最差X%設施的平均排放強度。應在依據第7條第7項公布的施行法確定X的值，且應在適當的程度確定X的值，以確保CBAM的環境完整性、以最新及可靠的資料為基礎，包括在過渡時期收集到的資料在內。

4.2. 第7條第3項進口電力的默認值

應根據第三國、第三國群組或第三國內一地區依據第4.2.1點規定的具體默認值確定，或若無法使用這些默認值時，則根據第4.2.2點規定替代的默認值確定進口電力的默認值。

若在第三國、第三國群組或第三國內一地區生產電力時，並為進口至歐盟的目的而過境第三國、第三國群組或第三國內地區或會員國時，所使用的默認值是電力生產的第三國、第三國群組或第三國內地區產生的默認值。

4.2.1. 對第三國、第三國群組或在第三國內一地區的具體默認值

應依據在第三國、第三國群組或在第三國內一地區依據執委會可取得最佳數據規定二氧化碳排放係數確定具體的默認值。

4.2.2. 替代的默認值

若對第三國、第三國群組或在第三國內一地區無可用的具體默認值時，應按在歐盟的二氧化碳排放係數確定電力的替代默認值。

若基於可靠資料得顯示在第三國、第三國群組或在第三國內一地區的二氧化碳排放係數低於由執委會確定的具體默認值或低於在歐盟內的二氧化碳排放係數時，則依據該二氧化碳排放係數的替代默認值得使用於該第三國、第三國群組或在第三國內一地區。

4.3. 間接內含排放量的默認值

在第三國生產的產品內含間接排放應由歐盟電網排放係

數、原產國電網排放係數或在原產國使用該產品電力定價來源的二氧化碳排放係數平均計算的默認值確定默認值。

第三國或一個第三國群組向執委會表述基於可靠的數據，在第三國或第三國群組平均電力組合排放係數或定價來源的二氧化碳排放係數低於間接排放的默認值時，應對此一第三國或第三國群組建立一個基於該平均二氧化碳排放係數的替代默認值。

不遲於2025年6月30日，執委會應依據第7條第7項規定公布一個施行法，以更進一步具體規定依據第1項應適用計算默認值，確定默認值的計算方法。為該目的，執委會自己應基於最新及可靠的數據，包括在過渡時期間收集到的資料在內，針對使用於附件一清單表列的產品生產的電量、以及關於這些電力的原產國、發電來源與排放係數。應基於最適當的方式確定具體的計算方法，以達到下列的兩個標準：

— 防止碳洩漏；

— 確保CBAM的環境完整性。

5. 適用在進口電力實際內含排放量的條件

若下列的標準全部符合時，經核准的CBAM申報人得適用實際內含排放量，取代以第7條第3項規定計算默認值：

(a) 在經核准的CBAM申報人與位於第三國的電力生產商簽訂了購電協議，涵蓋所主張使用實際內含排放量的電量；

(b) 電力生產的設施直接連結到歐盟的輸電系統或得顯示在出口時，在設施與歐盟輸電系統間的網絡任何點都無實體的網絡擁塞；

(c) 電力生產的設施排放不超過每千瓦時電力的化石燃料源的550g二氧化碳；

(d) 在原產國、目的國與若有相關的每個過境國所有負責輸電系統的營運商堅定主張所使用實際內含排放量的電量，指定分配的互連容量，且指定的容量與由設施生產的電力在同一時段不應超過一小時；

(e) 由一位經認可的查核人認證符合上述的標準，查核人應至少每月收到期中報告，說明是如何履行這些標準。

購電協議的累計電量與其相當的實際內含排放量不應算入國家排放係數或依據第4.3點為了使用於計算產品間接電力內含排放量的二氧化碳排放係數。

6. 對間接排放適用實際內含排放量的條件

若得說明在進口產品進行生產的設施與發電來源間有直接的技術連結或該設施的營運商與位於第三國的電力生產商對相等於主張使用具體電量，締結一個購電協議時，經核准的CBAM申報人得適用實際內含排放量，取代以第7條第4項規定計算默認值。

7. 根據第7條第2項規定的區域特定特徵調整默認值

可以根據在第三國內特別區域及地區的特別特徵所具有客觀排放係數，調整默認值。若可取得這些特定本地特徵調整的數據時，且可以確定數個針對性的默認值時，得使用後者。

來自第三國或第三國群組或在第三國內一地區的產品申報人，可以根據可靠數據，說明替代區域特定的默認值調整低於執委會確定的默認值時，可以使用區域特定的調整。

為第7條第5項的目的
計算內含排放量所使用資料的簿記要求

1. **對進口產品，經核准CBAM申報人應有的基本資料：**

   (1) 經核准CBAM申報人的身份資料：

   　　(a) 姓名；

   　　(b) CBAM帳號。

   (2) 進口產品的資料：

   　　(a) 每種產品的類型與數量；

   　　(b) 原產國；

   　　(c) 實際排放量或默認值。

2. **對在進口產品依據實際排放量確定的內含排放量，由經核准CBAM申報人應保存的基本資料：**

   　　對每個依據實際排放量確定的內含排放量的進口產品類型，應保存下列額外的資料：

   　　(a) 生產產品設施之辨識；

   　　(b) 生產產品設施營運商的聯絡資料；

   　　(c) 附件六的查證報告；

   　　(d) 產品具體的內含排放量。

為第8條的目的，
查證原則與查證報告的內容

1. 查證原則

應適用下列的原則：

(a) 查證人應以專業訊問的態度進行查證；

(b) 僅在查證人有合理保證認為查證報告無重大的錯誤陳述
與重大不符合附件四內含排放量計算的規則，在CBAM
申報應申報的內含排放總量應視為經查證；

(c) 查證人應進行實地查廠，但符合捨棄查廠特別標準者，
不在此限；

(d) 為決定錯誤陳述或不合規是否重大時，查證人應使用依
據第8條第3項公布施行法規定的門檻值。

對於未確定這些門檻值的參數，查證人應使用專家判斷，
根據其規模和性質證明，錯誤陳述或不合規單獨或與其他錯誤
陳述或不合規加總，確定錯誤陳述或不合規是否是為重大。

2. 查證報告內容

查證人應準備一個確定產品內含排放量，並指定與進
行查證工作相關所有議題的查證報告，至少應包括下列的
資料：

(a) 產品生產的設施辨識；

(b) 產品生產的設施營運商的聯絡資料；

(c) 適用申報的期限；

(d) 查證人的姓名與聯絡資料；

(e) 查證人的認證號碼與認證機構的名稱；

(f) 查廠的日期，或適用時，未進行查廠的理由；

(g) 在申報的期限所申報每種類型產品的數量；

(h) 在申報期間設施量化的直接排放；

(i) 描述設施的排放如何歸屬於產品不同的類型；

(j) 關於產品、排放與和這些產品無關的能源流動的數量資料；

(k) 在複雜產品的情形：

    (i) 使用的每個投入材料（前體）的數量；

    (ii) 與使用的每種投入材料（前體）相關的具體內含排放量；

    (iii)若使用實際排放量：生產投入材料（前體）與從該材料生產產生實際排放量的設施辨識；

(l) 查證人說明有合理保證確認報告無重大錯誤陳述與無重大不符合附件四的計算規則；

(m)發現重大錯誤陳述與更正的資料；

(n) 發現重大不符合附件四規定的計算規則與更正的資料。

PART **3**

CBAM 英文條文

REGULATION (EU) 2023/956 OF THE
EUROPEAN PARLIAMENT AND OF THE
COUNCIL of 10 May 2023

establishing a carbon border adjustment
mechanism

CHAPTER I

SUBJECT MATTER, SCOPE AND DEFINITIONS

Article 1

Subject matter

1. This Regulation establishes a carbon border adjustment mechanism (the 'CBAM') to address greenhouse gas emissions embedded in the goods listed in Annex I on their importation into the customs territory of the Union in order to prevent the risk of carbon leakage, thereby reducing global carbon emissions and supporting the goals of the Paris Agreement, also by creating incentives for the reduction of emissions by operators in third countries.

2. The CBAM complements the system for greenhouse gas emission allowance trading within the Union established under Directive 2003/87/EC (the 'EU ETS') by applying an equivalent set of rules to imports into the customs territory of the Union of the goods referred to in Article 2 of this Regulation.

3. The CBAM is set to replace the mechanisms established under Directive 2003/87/EC to prevent the risk of carbon leakage by reflecting the extent to which EU ETS allowances are allocated free of charge in accordance with Article 10a of that Directive.

Article 2

Scope

1. This Regulation applies to goods listed in Annex I originating in a third country, where those goods, or processed products from those goods resulting from the inward processing procedure referred to in Article 256 of Regulation (EU) No 952/2013, are imported into the customs territory of the Union.

2. This Regulation also applies to goods listed in Annex I to this Regulation originating in a third country, where those goods, or processed products from those goods resulting from the inward processing procedure referred to in Article 256 of Regulation (EU) No 952/2013, are brought to an artificial island, a fixed or floating structure, or any other structure on the continental shelf or in the exclusive economic zone of a Member State that is adjacent to the customs territory of the Union.

   The Commission shall adopt implementing acts laying down detailed conditions for the application of the CBAM to such goods, in particular as regards the notions equivalent to those of importation into the customs territory of the Union and of release for free circulation, as regards the procedures relating to the submission of the CBAM declaration in respect of such goods and the controls to be carried out by customs authorities. Those implementing acts shall be adopted in accordance with the examination procedure referred to in Article 29(2) of this Regulation.

3. By way of derogation from paragraphs 1 and 2, this Regulation shall not apply to:

   (a) goods listed in Annex I to this Regulation which are imported into the customs territory of the Union provided that the intrinsic value of such goods does not exceed, per consignment, the value specified for goods of negligible value as referred to in Article 23 of Council Regulation (EC) No 1186/2009 [1];

   (b) goods contained in the personal luggage of travellers coming from a third country provided that the intrinsic value of such goods does not exceed the value specified for goods of negligible value as referred to in Article 23 of Regulation (EC) No 1186/2009;

   (c) goods to be moved or used in the context of military activities pursuant to Article 1, point (49), of Commission Delegated Regulation (EU) 2015/2446 [2].

---

1 Council Regulation (EC) No 1186/2009 of 16 November 2009 setting up a Community system of reliefs from customs duty (OJ L 324, 10.12.2009, p. 23).

2 Commission Delegated Regulation (EU) 2015/2446 of 28 July 2015 supplementing Regulation (EU) No 952/2013 of the European Parliament and of the Council as regards detailed rules concerning certain provisions

4. By way of derogation from paragraphs 1 and 2, this Regulation shall not apply to goods originating in the third countries and territories listed in point 1 of Annex III.

5. Imported goods shall be considered as originating in third countries in accordance with the rules for non-preferential origin as referred to in Article 59 of Regulation (EU) No 952/2013.

6. Third countries and territories shall be listed in point 1 of Annex III where they fulfil all the following conditions:

    (a) the EU ETS applies to that third country or territory or an agreement has been concluded between that third country or territory and the Union fully linking the EU ETS and the emission trading system of that third country or territory;

    (b) the carbon price paid in the country in which the goods originate is effectively charged on the greenhouse gas emissions embedded in those goods without any rebates beyond those also applied in accordance with the EU ETS.

7. If a third country or territory has an electricity market which is integrated with the Union internal market for electricity through market coupling, and there is no technical solution for the application of the CBAM to the importation of electricity into the customs territory of the Union from that third country or territory,

---

of the Union Customs Code (OJ L 343, 29.12.2015, p. 1).

such importation of electricity from that country or territory shall be exempt from the application of the CBAM, provided that the Commission has assessed that all of the following conditions have been fulfilled in accordance with paragraph 8:

(a) the third country or territory has concluded an agreement with the Union which sets out an obligation to apply Union law in the field of electricity, including the legislation on the development of renewable energy sources, as well as other rules in the field of energy, environment and competition;

(b) the domestic legislation in that third country or territory implements the main provisions of Union electricity market legislation, including on the development of renewable energy sources and the market coupling of electricity markets;

(c) the third country or territory has submitted a roadmap to the Commission which contains a timetable for the adoption of measures to implement the conditions set out in points (d) and (e);

(d) the third country or territory has committed to climate neutrality by 2050 and, where applicable, has accordingly formally formulated and communicated to the United Nations Framework Convention on Climate Change (UNFCCC) a mid-century, long-term low greenhouse gas emissions development strategy aligned with that objective, and has implemented that commitment in its domestic legislation;

(e) the third country or territory has, when implementing the roadmap referred to in point (c), demonstrated its fulfilment of the set deadlines and the substantial progress towards the alignment of domestic legislation with Union law in the field of climate action on the basis of that roadmap, including towards carbon pricing at a level equivalent to that in the Union in particular insofar as the generation of electricity is concerned; the implementation of an emissions trading system for electricity, with a price equivalent to the EU ETS, is to be finalised by 1 January 2030;

(f) the third country or territory has put in place an effective system to prevent indirect import of electricity into the Union from other third countries or territories that do not fulfil the conditions set out in points (a) to (e).

8. A third country or territory that fulfils all the conditions set out in paragraph 7, shall be listed in point 2 of Annex III, and shall submit two reports on the fulfilment of those conditions, the first report by 1 July 2025 and the second by 31 December 2027. By 31 December 2025 and by 1 July 2028, the Commission shall assess, in particular on the basis of the roadmap referred to in paragraph 7, point (c), and the reports received from the third country or territory, if that third country or territory continues to

fulfil the conditions set out in paragraph 7.

9. A third country or territory listed in point 2 of Annex III shall be removed from that list where one or more of the following conditions applies:

(a) the Commission has reasons to consider that that third country or territory has not shown sufficient progress to comply with one of the conditions set out in paragraph 7, or that third country or territory has taken action that is incompatible with the objectives set out in the Union climate and environmental legislation;

(b) that third country or territory has taken steps that are contrary to its decarbonisation objectives, such as providing public support for the establishment of new generation capacity that emits more than 550 grammes of carbon dioxide ('CO_2') of fossil fuel origin per kilowatt-hour of electricity;

(c) the Commission has evidence that, as a result of increased exports of electricity to the Union, the emissions per kilowatt-hour of electricity produced in that third country or territory have increased by at least 5 % compared to 1 January 2026.

10. The Commission is empowered to adopt delegated acts in accordance with Article 28 in order to supplement this Regulation by laying down requirements and procedures for third countries or territories that have been removed from the list in point 2 of

歐盟CBAM法規：台灣廠商因應之道與申報準備

Annex III, to ensure the application of this Regulation to those countries or territories with regard to electricity. If in such cases market coupling remains incompatible with the application of this Regulation, the Commission may decide to exclude those third countries or territories from Union market coupling and require explicit capacity allocation at the border between the Union and those third countries or territories, so that the CBAM can apply.

11. The Commission is empowered to adopt delegated acts in accordance with Article 28 in order to amend the lists of third countries or territories listed in point 1 or 2 of Annex III by adding or removing a third country or territory, depending on whether the conditions set out in paragraph 6, 7 or 9 of this Article are fulfilled in respect of that third country or territory.

12. The Union may conclude agreements with third countries or territories with a view to taking into account carbon pricing mechanisms in such countries or territories for the purposes of the application of Article 9.

Article 3
Definitions

For the purposes of this Regulation, the following definitions apply:

(1) 'goods' means goods listed in Annex I;

(2) 'greenhouse gases' means greenhouse gases as specified in Annex I in relation to each of the goods listed in that Annex;

(3) 'emissions' means the release of greenhouse gases into the atmosphere from the production of goods;

(4) 'importation' means release for free circulation as provided for in Article 201 of Regulation (EU) No 952/2013;

(5) 'EU ETS' means the system for greenhouse gas emissions allowance trading within the Union in respect of activities listed in Annex I to Directive 2003/87/EC other than aviation activities;

(6) 'customs territory of the Union' means the territory defined in Article 4 of Regulation (EU) No 952/2013;

(7) 'third country' means a country or territory outside the customs territory of the Union;

(8) 'continental shelf' means a continental shelf as defined in Article 76 of the United Nations Convention on the Law of the Sea;

(9) 'exclusive economic zone' means an exclusive economic zone as defined in Article 55 of the United Nations Convention on the Law of the Sea and which has been declared as an exclusive economic zone by a Member State pursuant to that convention;

(10) 'intrinsic value' means the intrinsic value for commercial goods as defined in Article 1, point (48), of Delegated Regulation (EU) 2015/2446;

(11) 'market coupling' means the allocation of transmission capacity through a Union system which simultaneously matches orders and allocates cross-zonal capacities as set out in Regulation (EU) 2015/1222;

(12) 'explicit capacity allocation' means the allocation of cross-border transmission capacity separate from the trade of electricity;

(13) 'competent authority' means the authority designated by each Member State in accordance with Article 11;

(14) 'customs authorities' means the customs administrations of Member States as defined in Article 5, point (1), of Regulation (EU) No 952/2013;

(15) 'importer' means either the person lodging a customs declaration for release for free circulation of goods in its own name and on its own behalf or, where the customs declaration is lodged by an indirect customs representative in accordance with Article 18 of Regulation (EU) No 952/2013, the person on whose behalf such a declaration is lodged;

(16) 'customs declarant' means a declarant as defined in Article 5, point (15), of Regulation (EU) No 952/2013 lodging a customs declaration for release for free circulation of goods in its own name or the person in whose name such a declaration is lodged;

(17) 'authorised CBAM declarant' means a person authorised by a competent authority in accordance with Article 17;

(18) 'person' means a natural person, a legal person or any association of persons which is not a legal person but which is recognised under Union or national law as having the capacity to perform legal acts;

(19) 'established in a Member State' means:

(a) in the case of a natural person, any person whose place of residence is in a Member State;

(b) in the case of a legal person or an association of persons, any person whose registered office, central headquarters or permanent business establishment is in a Member State;

(20) 'Economic Operators Registration and Identification number (EORI number)' means the number assigned by the customs authority when the registration for customs purposes has been carried out in accordance with Article 9 of Regulation (EU) No 952/2013;

(21) 'direct emissions' means emissions from the production processes of goods, including emissions from the production of heating and cooling that is consumed during the production processes, irrespective of the location of the production of the heating or cooling;

(22) 'embedded emissions' means direct emissions released during the production of goods and indirect emissions from the production of electricity that is consumed during the production processes,

calculated in accordance with the methods set out in Annex IV and further specified in the implementing acts adopted pursuant to Article 7(7);

(23) 'tonne of CO_2e' means one metric tonne of CO_2, or an amount of any other greenhouse gas listed in Annex I with an equivalent global warming potential;

(24) 'CBAM certificate' means a certificate in electronic format corresponding to one tonne of CO_2e of embedded emissions in goods;

(25) 'surrender' means offsetting of CBAM certificates against the declared embedded emissions in imported goods or against the embedded emissions in imported goods that should have been declared;

(26) 'production processes' means the chemical and physical processes carried out to produce goods in an installation;

(27) 'default value' means a value, which is calculated or drawn from secondary data, which represents the embedded emissions in goods;

(28) 'actual emissions' means the emissions calculated based on primary data from the production processes of goods and from the production of electricity consumed during those processes as determined in accordance with the methods set out in Annex IV;

(29) 'carbon price' means the monetary amount paid in a third

country, under a carbon emissions reduction scheme, in the form of a tax, levy or fee or in the form of emission allowances under a greenhouse gas emissions trading system, calculated on greenhouse gases covered by such a measure, and released during the production of goods;

(30) 'installation' means a stationary technical unit where a production process is carried out;

(31) 'operator' means any person who operates or controls an installation in a third country;

(32) 'national accreditation body' means a national accreditation body as appointed by each Member State pursuant to Article 4(1) of Regulation (EC) No 765/2008;

(33) 'EU ETS allowance' means an allowance as defined in Article 3, point (a), of Directive 2003/87/EC in respect of activities listed in Annex I to that Directive other than aviation activities;

(34) 'indirect emissions' means emissions from the production of electricity which is consumed during the production processes of goods, irrespective of the location of the production of the consumed electricity.

CHAPTER II

OBLIGATIONS AND RIGHTS OF AUTHORISED CBAM DECLARANTS

Article 4

Importation of goods

Goods shall be imported into the customs territory of the Union only by an authorised CBAM declarant.

Article 5

Application for authorization

1. Any importer established in a Member State shall, prior to importing goods into the customs territory of the Union, apply for the status of authorised CBAM declarant ('application for an authorisation'). Where such an importer appoints an indirect customs representative in accordance with Article 18 of Regulation (EU) No 952/2013 and the indirect customs representative agrees to act as an authorised CBAM declarant, the indirect customs representative shall submit the application for an authorisation.

2. Where an importer is not established in a Member State, the indirect customs representative shall submit the application for an authorisation.

3. The application for an authorisation shall be submitted via the CBAM registry established in accordance with Article 14.

4. By way of derogation from paragraph 1, where transmission capacity for the import of electricity is allocated through explicit capacity allocation, the person to whom capacity has been allocated for import and who nominates that capacity for import shall, for the purposes of this Regulation, be regarded as an authorised CBAM declarant in the Member State where the person has declared the importation of electricity in the customs declaration. Imports are to be measured per border for time periods no longer than one hour and no deduction of export or transit in the same hour shall be possible.

   The competent authority of the Member State in which the customs declaration has been lodged shall register the person in the CBAM registry.

5. The application for an authorisation shall include the following information about the applicant:

   (a) name, address and contact information;

   (b) EORI number;

   (c) main economic activity carried out in the Union;

   (d) certification by the tax authority in the Member State where the applicant is established that the applicant is not subject to an outstanding recovery order for national tax debts;

(e) declaration of honour that the applicant was not involved in any serious infringements or repeated infringements of customs legislation, taxation rules or market abuse rules during the five years preceding the year of the application, including that it has no record of serious criminal offences relating to its economic activity;

(f) information necessary to demonstrate the applicant's financial and operational capacity to fulfil its obligations under this Regulation and, if decided by the competent authority on the basis of a risk assessment, supporting documents confirming that information, such as the profit and loss account and the balance sheet for up to the last three financial years for which the accounts were closed;

(g) estimated monetary value and volume of imports of goods into the customs territory of the Union by type of goods, for the calendar year during which the application is submitted, and for the following calendar year;

(h) names and contact information of the persons on behalf of whom the applicant is acting, if applicable.

6. The applicant may withdraw its application at any time.

7. The authorised CBAM declarant shall inform without delay the competent authority, via the CBAM registry, of any changes to the information provided under paragraph 5 of this Article that have

occurred after the decision granting the status of the authorised CBAM declarant has been adopted pursuant to Article 17 that may influence that decision or the content of the authorisation granted thereunder.

8. The Commission is empowered to adopt implementing acts on communications between the applicant, the competent authority and the Commission, on the standard format of the application for an authorisation and the procedures to submit such an application via the CBAM registry, on the procedure to be followed by the competent authority and the deadlines for processing applications for authorisation in accordance with paragraph 1 of this Article, and on the rules for identification by the competent authority of the authorised CBAM declarants for the importation of electricity. Those implementing acts shall be adopted in accordance with the examination procedure referred to in Article 29(2).

Article 6
CBAM declaration

1. By 31 May of each year, and for the first time in 2027 for the year 2026, each authorised CBAM declarant shall use the CBAM registry referred to in Article 14 to submit a CBAM declaration for

the preceding calendar year.

2. The CBAM declaration shall contain the following information:

   (a) the total quantity of each type of goods imported during the preceding calendar year, expressed in megawatt-hours for electricity and in tonnes for other goods;

   (b) the total embedded emissions in the goods referred to in point (a) of this paragraph, expressed in tonnes of CO_2e emissions per megawatt-hour of electricity or, for other goods, in tonnes of CO_2e emissions per tonne of each type of goods, calculated in accordance with Article 7 and verified in accordance with Article 8;

   (c) the total number of CBAM certificates to be surrendered, corresponding to the total embedded emissions referred to in point (b) of this paragraph after the reduction that is due on the account of the carbon price paid in a country of origin in accordance with Article 9 and the adjustment necessary to reflect the extent to which EU ETS allowances are allocated free of charge in accordance with Article 31;

   (d) copies of verification reports, issued by accredited verifiers, under Article 8 and Annex VI.

3. Where processed products resulting from an inward processing procedure as referred to in Article 256 of Regulation (EU) No 952/2013 are imported, the authorised CBAM declarant shall

report in the CBAM declaration the emissions embedded in the goods that were placed under the inward processing procedure and resulted in the imported processed products, even where the processed products are not goods listed in Annex I to this Regulation. This paragraph shall also apply where the processed products resulting from the inward processing procedure are returned goods as referred to in Article 205 of Regulation (EU) No 952/2013.

4. Where the imported goods listed in Annex I to this Regulation are processed products resulting from an outward processing procedure as referred to in Article 259 of Regulation (EU) No 952/2013, the authorised CBAM declarant shall report in the CBAM declaration only the emissions of the processing operation undertaken outside the customs territory of the Union.

5. Where the imported goods are returned goods as referred to in Article 203 of Regulation (EU) No 952/2013, the authorised CBAM declarant shall report separately, in the CBAM declaration, 'zero' for the total embedded emissions corresponding to those goods.

6. The Commission is empowered to adopt implementing acts concerning the standard format of the CBAM declaration, including detailed information for each installation and country of origin and type of goods to be reported which supports the totals

referred to in paragraph 2 of this Article, in particular as regards embedded emissions and carbon price paid, the procedure for submitting the CBAM declaration via the CBAM registry, and the arrangements for surrendering the CBAM certificates referred to in paragraph 2, point (c), of this Article, in accordance with Article 22(1), in particular as regards the process and the selection by the authorised CBAM declarant of certificates to be surrendered. Those implementing acts shall be adopted in accordance with the examination procedure referred to in Article 29(2).

Article 7
Calculation of embedded emissions

1. Embedded emissions in goods shall be calculated pursuant to the methods set out in Annex IV. For goods listed in Annex II only direct emissions shall be calculated and taken into account.

2. Embedded emissions in goods other than electricity shall be determined based on the actual emissions in accordance with the methods set out in points 2 and 3 of Annex IV. Where the actual emissions cannot be adequately determined, as well as in the case of indirect emissions, the embedded emissions shall be determined by reference to default values in accordance with the methods set

out in point 4.1 of Annex IV.

3. Embedded emissions in imported electricity shall be determined by reference to default values in accordance with the method set out in point 4.2 of Annex IV, unless the authorised CBAM declarant demonstrates that the criteria to determine the embedded emissions based on the actual emissions listed in point 5 of Annex IV are met.

4. Embedded indirect emissions shall be calculated in accordance with the method set out in point 4.3 of Annex IV and further specified in the implementing acts adopted pursuant to paragraph 7 of this Article, unless the authorised CBAM declarant demonstrates that the criteria to determine the embedded emissions based on actual emissions that are listed in point 6 of Annex IV are met.

5. The authorised CBAM declarant shall keep records of the information required to calculate the embedded emissions in accordance with the requirements laid down in Annex V. Those records shall be sufficiently detailed to enable verifiers accredited pursuant to Article 18 to verify the embedded emissions in accordance with Article 8 and Annex VI and to enable the Commission and the competent authority to review the CBAM declaration in accordance with Article 19(2).

6. The authorised CBAM declarant shall keep those records of

information referred to in paragraph 5, including the report of the verifier, until the end of the fourth year after the year in which the CBAM declaration has been or should have been submitted.

7. The Commission is empowered to adopt implementing acts concerning:

(a) the application of the elements of the calculation methods set out in Annex IV, including determining system boundaries of production processes and relevant input materials (precursors), emission factors, installation-specific values of actual emissions and default values and their respective application to individual goods as well as laying down methods to ensure the reliability of data on the basis of which the default values shall be determined, including the level of detail and the verification of the data, and including further specification of goods that are to be considered as 'simple goods' and 'complex goods' for the purpose of point 1 of Annex IV; those implementing acts shall also specify the conditions under which it is deemed that actual emissions cannot be adequately determined, as well as the elements of evidence demonstrating that the criteria required to justify the use of actual emissions for electricity consumed in the production processes of goods for the purpose of paragraph 2 that are listed in points 5 and 6 of Annex IV are met; and

(b) the application of the elements of the calculation methods pursuant to paragraph 4 in accordance with point 4.3 of Annex IV.

Where objectively justified, the implementing acts referred to in the first subparagraph shall provide that default values can be adapted to particular areas, regions or countries to take into account specific objective factors that affect emissions, such as prevailing energy sources or industrial processes. Those implementing acts shall build upon existing legislation for the monitoring and verification of emissions and activity data for installations covered by Directive 2003/87/EC, in particular Commission Implementing Regulation (EU) 2018/2066 [3], Implementing Regulation (EU) 2018/2067 and Commission Delegated Regulation (EU) 2019/331 [4]. Those implementing acts shall be adopted in accordance with the examination procedure referred to in Article 29(2) of this Regulation.

---

3 Commission Implementing Regulation (EU) 2018/2066 of 19 December 2018 on the monitoring and reporting of greenhouse gas emissions pursuant to Directive 2003/87/EC of the European Parliament and of the Council and amending Commission Regulation (EU) No 601/2012 (OJ L 334, 31.12.2018, p. 1).

4 Commission Delegated Regulation (EU) 2019/331 of 19 December 2018 determining transitional Union-wide rules for harmonised free allocation of emission allowances pursuant to Article 10a of Directive 2003/87/EC of the European Parliament and of the Council (OJ L 59, 27.2.2019, p. 8).

Article 8

Verification of embedded emissions

1. The authorised CBAM declarant shall ensure that the total embedded emissions declared in the CBAM declaration submitted pursuant to Article 6 are verified by a verifier accredited pursuant to Article 18, based on the verification principles set out in Annex VI.

2. For embedded emissions in goods produced in installations in a third country registered in accordance with Article 10, the authorised CBAM declarant may choose to use verified information disclosed to it in accordance with Article 10(7) to fulfil the obligation referred to in paragraph 1 of this Article.

3. The Commission is empowered to adopt implementing acts for the application of the verification principles set out in Annex VI as regards:

   (a) the possibility to waive, in duly justified circumstances and without putting at risk a reliable estimation of the embedded emissions, the obligation for the verifier to visit the installation where relevant goods are produced;

   (b) the definition of thresholds for deciding whether misstatements or non-conformities are material; and

   (c) the supporting documentation needed for the verification report, including its format.

Where it adopts the implementing acts referred to in the first subparagraph, the Commission shall seek equivalence and coherence with the procedures set out in Implementing Regulation (EU) 2018/2067. Those implementing acts shall be adopted in accordance with the examination procedure referred to in Article 29(2) of this Regulation.

Article 9
Carbon price paid in a third country

1. An authorised CBAM declarant may claim in the CBAM declaration a reduction in the number of CBAM certificates to be surrendered in order to take into account the carbon price paid in the country of origin for the declared embedded emissions. The reduction may be claimed only if the carbon price has been effectively paid in the country of origin. In such a case, any rebate or other form of compensation available in that country that would have resulted in a reduction of that carbon price shall be taken into account.

2. The authorised CBAM declarant shall keep records of the documentation required to demonstrate that the declared embedded emissions were subject to a carbon price in the country

歐盟CBAM法規：台灣廠商因應之道與申報準備

of origin of the goods that has been effectively paid as referred to in paragraph 1. The authorised CBAM declarant shall in particular keep evidence related to any rebate or other form of compensation available, in particular the references to the relevant legislation of that country. The information contained in that documentation shall be certified by a person that is independent from the authorised CBAM declarant and from the authorities of the country of origin. The name and contact information of that independent person shall appear on the documentation. The authorised CBAM declarant shall also keep evidence of the actual payment of the carbon price.

3. The authorised CBAM declarant shall keep the records referred to in paragraph 2 until the end of the fourth year after the year during which the CBAM declaration has been or should have been submitted.

4. The Commission is empowered to adopt implementing acts concerning the conversion of the yearly average carbon price effectively paid in accordance with paragraph 1 into a corresponding reduction of the number of CBAM certificates to be surrendered, including the conversion of the carbon price effectively paid in foreign currency into euro at the yearly average exchange rate, the evidence required of the actual payment of the carbon price, examples of any relevant rebate or other form of

compensation referred to in paragraph 1 of this Article, the qualifications of the independent person referred to in paragraph 2 of this Article and the conditions to ascertain that person's independence. Those implementing acts shall be adopted in accordance with the examination procedure referred to in Article 29(2).

Article 10
Registration of operators and of installations in third countries

1. The Commission shall, upon request by an operator of an installation located in a third country, register the information on that operator and on its installation in the CBAM registry referred to in Article 14.

2. The request for registration referred to in paragraph 1 shall contain the following information to be included in the CBAM registry upon registration:

   (a) the name, address and contact information of the operator;

   (b) the location of each installation including the complete address and geographical coordinates expressed in longitude and latitude, including six decimals;

   (c) the main economic activity of the installation.

3. The Commission shall notify the operator of the registration in the

CBAM registry. The registration shall be valid for a period of five years from the date of its notification to the operator of the installation.

4. The operator shall inform the Commission without delay of any changes in the information referred to in paragraph 2 arising after the registration, and the Commission shall update the relevant information in the CBAM registry.

5. The operator shall:

(a) determine the embedded emissions calculated in accordance with the methods set out in Annex IV, by type of goods produced at the installation referred to in paragraph 1 of this Article;

(b) ensure that the embedded emissions referred to in point (a) of this paragraph are verified in accordance with the verification principles set out in Annex VI by a verifier accredited pursuant to Article 18;

(c) keep a copy of the verification report as well as records of the information required to calculate the embedded emissions in goods in accordance with the requirements laid down in Annex V for a period of four years after the verification has been performed.

6. The records referred to in paragraph 5, point (c), of this Article shall be sufficiently detailed to enable the verification of the

embedded emissions in accordance with Article 8 and Annex VI, and to enable the review, in accordance with Article 19, of the CBAM declaration made by an authorised CBAM declarant to whom the relevant information was disclosed in accordance with paragraph 7 of this Article.

7. An operator may disclose the information on the verification of embedded emissions referred to in paragraph 5 of this Article to an authorised CBAM declarant. The authorised CBAM declarant shall be entitled to use that disclosed information in order to fulfil the obligation referred to in Article 8.

8. The operator may, at any time, ask to be deregistered from the CBAM registry. The Commission shall, upon such request, and after notifying the competent authorities, deregister the operator and delete the information on that operator and on its installation from the CBAM registry, provided that such information is not necessary for the review of CBAM declarations that have been submitted. The Commission may, after having given the operator concerned the possibility to be heard and having consulted with the relevant competent authorities, also deregister the information if the Commission finds that the information on that operator is no longer accurate. The Commission shall inform the competent authorities of such deregistrations.

CHAPTER III

COMPETENT AUTHORITIES

Article 11

Competent authorities

1. Each Member State shall designate the competent authority to carry out the functions and duties under this Regulation and inform the Commission thereof.

   The Commission shall make available to the Member States a list of all competent authorities and publish that information in the *Official Journal of the European Union* and make that information available in the CBAM registry.

2. Competent authorities shall exchange any information that is essential or relevant to the exercise of their functions and duties under this Regulation.

Article 12

Commission

In addition to the other tasks that it exercises under this Regulation, the Commission shall assist the competent authorities in carrying out their functions and duties under this Regulation and shall coordinate their activities by supporting the exchange of, and issuing guidelines on, best practices within the scope of this Regulation, and by promoting an adequate exchange of information and cooperation between competent authorities as well as between competent authorities and the Commission.

Article 13
Professional secrecy and disclosure of information

1. All information acquired by the competent authority or the Commission in the course of performing their duties which is by its nature confidential or which is provided on a confidential basis shall be covered by the obligation of professional secrecy. Such information shall not be disclosed by the competent authority or the Commission without the express prior permission of the person or authority that provided it or by virtue of Union or national law.

2. By way of derogation from paragraph 1, the competent authorities and the Commission may share such information with each other, the customs authorities, the authorities in charge of administrative or criminal penalties, and the European Public Prosecutor's Office, for the purposes of ensuring compliance of persons with their obligations under this Regulation and the application of customs

legislation. Such shared information shall be covered by professional secrecy and shall not be disclosed to any other person or authority except by virtue of Union or national law.

Article 14
CBAM registry

1. The Commission shall establish a CBAM registry of authorised CBAM declarants in the form of a standardised electronic database containing the data regarding the CBAM certificates of those authorised CBAM declarants. The Commission shall make the information in the CBAM registry available automatically and in real time to customs authorities and competent authorities.

2. The CBAM registry referred to in paragraph 1 shall contain accounts with information about each authorised CBAM declarant, in particular:

   (a) the name, address and contact information of the authorised CBAM declarant;

   (b) the EORI number of the authorised CBAM declarant;

   (c) the CBAM account number;

   (d) the identification number, the sale price, the date of sale, and the date of surrender, repurchase or cancellation of CBAM certificates for each authorised CBAM declarant.

3. The CBAM registry shall contain, in a separate section of the registry, the information about the operators and installations in third countries registered in accordance with Article 10(2).

4. The information in the CBAM registry referred to in paragraphs 2 and 3 shall be confidential, with the exception of the names, addresses and contact information of the operators and the location of installations in third countries. An operator may choose not to have its name, address and contact information made accessible to the public. The public information in the CBAM registry shall be made accessible by the Commission in an interoperable format.

5. The Commission shall publish, on a yearly basis, for each of the goods listed in Annex I, the aggregated emissions embedded in the imported goods.

6. The Commission shall adopt implementing acts concerning the infrastructure and specific processes and procedures of the CBAM registry, including the risk analysis referred to in Article 15, the electronic databases containing the information referred to in paragraphs 2 and 3 of this Article, the data of the accounts in the CBAM registry referred to in Article 16, the transmission to the CBAM registry of the information on the sale, repurchase and cancellation of CBAM certificates referred to in Article 20, and the cross-check of information referred to in Article 25(3). Those

implementing acts shall be adopted in accordance with the examination procedure referred to in Article 29(2).

Article 15
Risk analysis

1. The Commission shall carry out risk-based controls on the data and the transactions recorded in the CBAM registry, referred to in Article 14, to ensure that there are no irregularities in the purchase, holding, surrender, repurchase and cancellation of CBAM certificates.

2. If the Commission identifies irregularities as a result of the controls carried out under paragraph 1, it shall inform the competent authorities concerned so that further investigations are carried out in order to correct the identified irregularities.

Article 16
Accounts in the CBAM registry

1. The Commission shall assign to each authorised CBAM declarant a unique CBAM account number.

2. Each authorised CBAM declarant shall be granted access to its account in the CBAM registry.

3. The Commission shall set up the account as soon as the authorisation referred to in Article 17(1) is granted and shall notify the authorised CBAM declarant thereof.

4. If the authorised CBAM declarant has ceased its economic activity or its authorisation has been revoked, the Commission shall close the account of that authorised CBAM declarant, provided that the authorised CBAM declarant has complied with all its obligations under this Regulation.

Article 17
Authorisation

1. Where an application for an authorisation is submitted in accordance with Article 5, the competent authority in the Member State in which the applicant is established shall grant the status of authorised CBAM declarant provided that the criteria set out in paragraph 2 of this Article are complied with. The status of authorised CBAM declarant shall be recognised in all Member States.

Before granting the status of authorised CBAM declarant, the competent authority shall conduct a consultation procedure on the application for an authorisation via the CBAM registry. The consultation procedure shall involve the competent authorities in

歐盟CBAM法規：台灣廠商因應之道與申報準備

the other Member States and the Commission and shall not exceed 15 working days.

2. The criteria for granting the status of authorised CBAM declarant shall be the following:

(a) the applicant has not been involved in a serious infringement or in repeated infringements of customs legislation, taxation rules, market abuse rules or this Regulation and delegated and implementing acts adopted under this Regulation, and in particular the applicant has no record of serious criminal offences relating to its economic activity during the five years preceding the application;

(b) the applicant demonstrates its financial and operational capacity to fulfil its obligations under this Regulation;

(c) the applicant is established in the Member State where the application is submitted; and

(d) the applicant has been assigned an EORI number in accordance with Article 9 of Regulation (EU) No 952/2013.

3. Where the competent authority finds that the criteria set out in paragraph 2 of this Article are not fulfilled, or where the applicant has failed to provide information listed in Article 5(5), the granting of the status of authorised CBAM declarant shall be refused. Such decision to refuse the status of authorised CBAM declarant shall provide the reasons for the refusal and include information on the

possibility to appeal.

4. A decision of the competent authority granting the status of authorised CBAM declarant shall be registered in the CBAM registry and shall contain the following information:

   (a) the name, address and contact information of the authorised CBAM declarant;

   (b) the EORI number of the authorised CBAM declarant;

   (c) the CBAM account number assigned to the authorised CBAM declarant in accordance with Article 16(1);

   (d) the guarantee required in accordance with paragraph 5 of this Article.

5. For the purpose of complying with the criteria set out in paragraph 2, point (b), of this Article, the competent authority shall require the provision of a guarantee if the applicant was not established throughout the two financial years preceding the year when the application in accordance with Article 5(1) was submitted.

   The competent authority shall fix the amount of such guarantee at the amount, calculated as the aggregate value of the number of CBAM certificates that the authorised CBAM declarant would have to surrender in accordance with Article 22 in respect of the imports of goods reported in accordance with Article 5(5), point (g). The guarantee provided shall be a bank guarantee, payable at first demand, by a financial institution operating in the Union or another form of guarantee which provides equivalent assurance.

6. Where the competent authority establishes that the guarantee provided does not ensure, or is no longer sufficient to ensure, the financial and operational capacity of the authorised CBAM declarant to fulfil its obligations under this Regulation, it shall require the authorised CBAM declarant to choose between providing an additional guarantee or replacing the initial guarantee with a new guarantee in accordance with paragraph 5.

7. The competent authority shall release the guarantee immediately after 31 May of the second year in which the authorised CBAM declarant has surrendered CBAM certificates in accordance with Article 22.

8. The competent authority shall revoke the status of authorised CBAM declarant where:

(a) the authorised CBAM declarant requests a revocation; or

(b) the authorised CBAM declarant no longer meets the criteria set out in paragraph 2 or 6 of this Article, or has been involved in a serious or repeated infringement of the obligation to surrender CBAM certificates referred to in Article 22(1) or of the obligation to ensure a sufficient number of CBAM certificates on its account in the CBAM registry at the end of each quarter referred to in Article 22(2).

Before revoking the status of authorised CBAM declarant, the competent authority shall give the authorised CBAM declarant the possibility to be heard and shall conduct a consultation procedure on the possible revocation of such status. The consultation procedure shall involve the competent authorities in the other Member States and the Commission and shall not exceed 15 working days.

Any decision of revocation shall contain the reasons for the decision as well as information about the right to appeal.

9. The competent authority shall register in the CBAM registry information on:

(a) the applicants whose application for an authorisation has been refused pursuant to paragraph 3; and

(b) the persons whose status of authorised CBAM declarant has been revoked pursuant to paragraph 8.

10. The Commission shall adopt, by means of implementing acts, the conditions for:

(a) the application of the criteria referred to in paragraph 2 of this Article, including that of not having been involved in a serious infringement or in repeated infringements under paragraph 2, point (a), of this Article;

(b) the application of the guarantee referred to in paragraphs 5, 6 and 7 of this Article;

(c) the application of the criteria of a serious or repeated infringement referred to in paragraph 8 of this Article;

(d) the consequences of the revocation of the status of authorised CBAM declarant referred to in paragraph 8 of this Article; and

(e) the specific deadlines and format of the consultation procedure referred to in paragraphs 1 and 8 of this Article.

The implementing acts referred to in the first subparagraph shall be adopted in accordance with the examination procedure referred to in Article 29(2).

Article 18
Accreditation of verifiers

1. Any person accredited in accordance with Implementing Regulation (EU) 2018/2067 for a relevant group of activities shall be an accredited verifier for the purpose of this Regulation. The Commission is empowered to adopt implementing acts to identify relevant groups of activities by providing an alignment of the qualifications of an accredited verifier that are necessary to perform verifications for the purpose of this Regulation with the relevant group of activities listed in Annex I to Implementing Regulation (EU) 2018/2067 and indicated in the accreditation certificate. Those implementing acts shall be adopted in accordance with the examination procedure referred to in Article 29(2) of this

Regulation.

2. A national accreditation body may, on request, accredit a person to be a verifier for the purpose of this Regulation where it considers, on the basis of the documentation submitted to it, that such person has the capacity to apply the verification principles referred to in Annex VI when performing the tasks of verification of the embedded emissions pursuant to Articles 8 and 10.

3. The Commission is empowered to adopt delegated acts in accordance with Article 28 in order to supplement this Regulation by specifying the conditions for granting of accreditation referred to in paragraph 2 of this Article, for the control and oversight of accredited verifiers, for the withdrawal of accreditation and for mutual recognition and peer evaluation of accreditation bodies.

Article 19
Review of CBAM declarations

1. The Commission shall have the oversight role in the review of CBAM declarations.

2. The Commission may review CBAM declarations, in accordance with a review strategy, including risk factors, within the period ending with the fourth year after the year during which the CBAM declarations should have been submitted.

歐盟CBAM法規：台灣廠商因應之道與申報準備

The review may consist in verifying the information provided in the CBAM declaration and in verification reports on the basis of the information communicated by the customs authorities in accordance with Article 25, any other relevant evidence, and on the basis of any audit deemed necessary, including at the premises of the authorised CBAM declarant.

The Commission shall communicate the initiation and the results of the review to the competent authority of the Member State where the CBAM declarant is established, via the CBAM registry.

The competent authority of the Member State where the authorised CBAM declarant is established may also review a CBAM declaration within the period referred to in the first subparagraph of this paragraph. The competent authority shall communicate the initiation and the results of a review to the Commission, via the CBAM registry.

3. The Commission shall periodically set out specific risk factors and points for attention, based on a risk analysis in relation to the implementation of the CBAM at Union level, taking into account information contained in the CBAM registry, data communicated by customs authorities, and other relevant information sources, including the controls and checks carried out pursuant to Article 15(2) and Article 25.

The Commission shall also facilitate the exchange of information with competent authorities about fraudulent activities and the penalties imposed in accordance with Article 26.

4. Where an authorised CBAM declarant fails to submit a CBAM declaration in accordance with Article 6, or where the Commission considers, on the basis of its review under paragraph 2 of this Article, that the declared number of CBAM certificates is incorrect, the Commission shall assess the obligations under this Regulation of that authorised CBAM declarant on the basis of the information at its disposal. The Commission shall establish a preliminary calculation of the total number of CBAM certificates which should have been surrendered, at the latest by the 31 December of the year following that in which the CBAM declaration should have been submitted, or at the latest by 31 December of the fourth year following that in which the incorrect CBAM declaration has been submitted, as applicable. The Commission shall provide to competent authorities such a preliminary calculation, for indicative purposes and without prejudice to the definitive calculation established by the competent authority of the Member State where the authorised CBAM declarant is established.

5. Where the competent authority concludes that the declared number of CBAM certificates to be surrendered is incorrect, or that no CBAM declaration has been submitted in accordance with

Article 6, it shall determine the number of CBAM certificates which should have been surrendered by the authorised CBAM declarant, taking into account the information submitted by the Commission.

The competent authority shall notify the authorised CBAM declarant of its decision on the number of CBAM certificates determined and shall request that the authorised CBAM declarant surrender the additional CBAM certificates within one month.

The competent authority's decision shall contain the reasons for the decision as well as information about the right to appeal. The decision shall also be notified via the CBAM registry.

Where the competent authority, after receiving the preliminary calculation from the Commission in accordance with paragraphs 2 and 4 of this Article, decides not to take any action, the competent authority shall inform the Commission accordingly, via the CBAM registry.

6. Where the competent authority concludes that the number of CBAM certificates surrendered exceeds the number which should have been surrendered, it shall inform the Commission without delay. The CBAM certificates surrendered in excess shall be repurchased in accordance with Article 23.

CHAPTER IV

CBAM CERTIFICATES

Article 20
Sale of CBAM certificates

1. A Member State shall sell CBAM certificates on a common central platform to authorised CBAM declarants established in that Member State.

2. The Commission shall establish and manage the common central platform following a joint procurement procedure between the Commission and the Member States.

The Commission and the competent authorities shall have access to the information in the common central platform.

3. The information on the sale, repurchase and cancellation of CBAM certificates in the common central platform shall be transferred to the CBAM registry at the end of each working day.

4. CBAM certificates shall be sold to authorised CBAM declarants at the price calculated in accordance with Article 21.

5. The Commission shall ensure that each CBAM certificate is assigned a unique identification number upon its creation. The Commission shall register the unique identification number and the price and date of sale of the CBAM certificate in the CBAM

registry in the account of the authorised CBAM declarant purchasing that certificate.

6. The Commission shall adopt delegated acts in accordance with Article 28 supplementing this Regulation by further specifying the timing, administration and other aspects related to the management of the sale and repurchase of CBAM certificates, seeking coherence with the procedures of Commission Regulation (EU) No 1031/2010 [5].

Article 21
Price of CBAM certificates

1. The Commission shall calculate the price of CBAM certificates as the average of the closing prices of EU ETS allowances on the auction platform, in accordance with the procedures laid down in Regulation (EU) No 1031/2010, for each calendar week.

For those calendar weeks in which no auctions are scheduled on the auction platform, the price of CBAM certificates shall be the

---

5 Commission Regulation (EU) No 1031/2010 of 12 November 2010 on the timing, administration and other aspects of auctioning of greenhouse gas emission allowances pursuant to Directive 2003/87/EC of the European Parliament and of the Council establishing a system for greenhouse gas emission allowances trading within the Union (OJ L 302, 18.11.2010, p. 1).

average of the closing prices of EU ETS allowances of the last week in which auctions on the auction platform took place.

2. The Commission shall publish the average price, as referred to in the second subparagraph of paragraph 1, on its website or in any other appropriate manner on the first working day of the following calendar week. That price shall apply from the first working day following that of its publication to the first working day of the following calendar week.

3. The Commission is empowered to adopt implementing acts on the application of the methodology provided for in paragraph 1 of this Article to calculate the average price of CBAM certificates and the practical arrangements for the publication of that price. Those implementing acts shall be adopted in accordance with the examination procedure referred to in Article 29(2).

Article 22
Surrender of CBAM certificates

1. By 31 May of each year, and for the first time in 2027 for the year 2026, the authorised CBAM declarant shall surrender via the CBAM registry a number of CBAM certificates that corresponds to the embedded emissions declared in accordance with Article 6(2), point (c), and verified in accordance with Article 8,

for the calendar year preceding the surrender. The Commission shall remove surrendered CBAM certificates from the CBAM registry. The authorised CBAM declarant shall ensure that the required number of CBAM certificates is available on its account in the CBAM registry.

2. The authorised CBAM declarant shall ensure that the number of CBAM certificates on its account in the CBAM registry at the end of each quarter corresponds to at least 80 % of the embedded emissions, determined by reference to default values in accordance with the methods set out in Annex IV, in all goods it has imported since the beginning of the calendar year.

3. Where the Commission finds that the number of CBAM certificates in the account of an authorised CBAM declarant does not comply with the obligations pursuant to paragraph 2, it shall inform, via the CBAM registry, the competent authority of the Member State where the authorised CBAM declarant is established.

The competent authority shall notify the authorised CBAM declarant of the need to ensure a sufficient number of CBAM certificates in its account within one month of such notification.

The competent authority shall register the notification to, and the response from, the authorised CBAM declarant in the CBAM registry.

Article 23

Repurchase of CBAM certificates

1. Where an authorised CBAM declarant so requests, the Member State where that authorised CBAM declarant is established shall repurchase the excess CBAM certificates remaining on the account of the declarant in the CBAM registry after the certificates have been surrendered in accordance with Article 22.

   The Commission shall repurchase the excess CBAM certificates through the common central platform referred to in Article 20 on behalf of the Member State where the authorised CBAM declarant is established. The authorised CBAM declarant shall submit the repurchase request by 30 June of each year during which CBAM certificates were surrendered.

2. The number of certificates subject to repurchase as referred to in paragraph 1 shall be limited to one third of the total number of CBAM certificates purchased by the authorised CBAM declarant during the previous calendar year.

3. The repurchase price for each CBAM certificate shall be the price paid by the authorised CBAM declarant for that certificate at the time of purchase.

Article 24
Cancellation of CBAM certificates

On 1 July of each year, the Commission shall cancel any CBAM certificates that were purchased during the year before the previous calendar year and that remained in the account of an authorised CBAM declarant in the CBAM registry. Those CBAM certificates shall be cancelled without any compensation.

Where the number of CBAM certificates to be surrendered is contested in a pending dispute in a Member State, the Commission shall suspend the cancellation of the CBAM certificates to the extent corresponding to the disputed amount. The competent authority of the Member State where the authorised CBAM declarant is established shall communicate without delay any relevant information to the Commission.

CHAPTER V

RULES APPLICABLE TO THE IMPORTATION OF GOODS

Article 25
Rules applicable to the importation of goods

1. The customs authorities shall not allow the importation of goods by any person other than an authorised CBAM declarant.

2. The customs authorities shall periodically and automatically, in particular by means of the surveillance mechanism established pursuant to Article 56(5) of Regulation (EU) No 952/2013, communicate to the Commission specific information on the goods declared for importation. That information shall include the EORI number and the CBAM account number of the authorised CBAM declarant, the eight-digit CN code of the goods, the quantity, the country of origin, the date of the customs declaration and the customs procedure.

3. The Commission shall communicate the information referred to in paragraph 2 of this Article to the competent authority of the Member State where the authorised CBAM declarant is established and shall, for each CBAM declarant, cross-check that information with the data in the CBAM registry pursuant to Article 14.

4. The customs authorities may communicate, in accordance with Article 12(1) of Regulation (EU) No 952/2013, confidential information acquired by the customs authorities in the course of performing their duties, or provided to the customs authorities on a confidential basis, to the Commission and the competent authority of the Member State that has granted the status of the authorised CBAM declarant.

5. Regulation (EC) No 515/97 shall apply *mutatis mutandis* to this Regulation.

6. The Commission is empowered to adopt implementing acts defining the scope of information and the periodicity, timing and means for communicating that information pursuant to paragraph 2 of this Article. Those implementing acts shall be adopted in accordance with the examination procedure referred to in Article 29(2).

CHAPTER VI

ENFORCEMENT

Article 26
Penalties

1. An authorised CBAM declarant who fails to surrender, by 31 May of each year, the number of CBAM certificates that corresponds to the emissions embedded in goods imported during the preceding calendar year shall be held liable for the payment of a penalty. Such a penalty shall be identical to the excess emissions penalty set out in Article 16(3) of Directive 2003/87/EC and increased pursuant to Article 16(4) of that Directive, applicable in the year of importation of the goods. Such a penalty shall apply for each CBAM certificate that the authorised CBAM declarant has not surrendered.

2. Where a person other than an authorised CBAM declarant introduces goods into the customs territory of the Union without complying with the obligations under this Regulation, that person shall be held liable for the payment of a penalty. Such a penalty shall be effective, proportionate and dissuasive and shall, depending in particular on the duration, gravity, scope, intentional nature and repetition of such non-compliance and the level of

cooperation of the person with the competent authority, be an amount from three to five times the penalty referred to in paragraph 1, applicable in the year of introduction of the goods, for each CBAM certificate that the person has not surrendered.

3. The payment of the penalty shall not release the authorised CBAM declarant from the obligation to surrender the outstanding number of CBAM certificates in a given year.

4. If the competent authority determines, including in light of the preliminary calculations made by the Commission in accordance with Article 19, that an authorised CBAM declarant has failed to comply with the obligation to surrender CBAM certificates as set out in paragraph 1 of this Article, or that a person has introduced goods into the customs territory of the Union without complying with the obligations under this Regulation as set out in paragraph 2 of this Article, the competent authority shall impose the penalty pursuant to paragraph 1 or 2 of this Article, as applicable. To that end, the competent authority shall notify the authorised CBAM declarant or, where paragraph 2 of this Article applies, the person:

(a) that the competent authority has concluded that the authorised CBAM declarant or the person referred to in paragraph 2 of this Article failed to comply with the obligations under this Regulation;

(b) of the reasons for its conclusion;

(c) of the amount of the penalty imposed on the authorised CBAM declarant or on the person referred to in paragraph 2 of this Article;

(d) of the date from which the penalty is due;

(e) of the action that the authorised CBAM declarant or the person referred to in paragraph 2 of this Article is to take to pay the penalty; and

(f) of the right of the authorised CBAM declarant or of the person referred to in paragraph 2 of this Article to appeal.

5. Where the penalty has not been paid by the due date referred to in paragraph 4, point (d), the competent authority shall secure payment of that penalty by all means available to it under the national law of the Member State concerned.

6. Member States shall communicate the decisions on penalties referred to in paragraphs 1 and 2 to the Commission and shall register the final payment referred to in paragraph 5 in the CBAM registry.

Article 27
Circumvention

1. The Commission shall take action in accordance with this Article, based on relevant and objective data, to address practices of

circumvention of this Regulation.

2. Practices of circumvention shall be defined as a change in the pattern of trade in goods, which stems from a practice, process or work, for which there is insufficient due cause or economic justification other than to avoid, wholly or partially, any of the obligations laid down in this Regulation. Such practice, process or work may consist of, but is not limited to:

(a) slightly modifying the goods concerned to make those goods fall under CN codes which are not listed in Annex I, except where the modification alters their essential characteristics;

(b) artificially splitting shipments into consignments the intrinsic value of which does not exceed the threshold referred to in Article 2(3).

3. The Commission shall continuously monitor the situation at Union level with a view to identifying practices of circumvention, including by way of market surveillance or on the basis of any relevant source of information, such as submissions by, and reporting from, civil society organisations.

4. A Member State or any party that has been affected by, or has benefited from, any of the situations referred to in paragraph 2 may notify the Commission if it is confronted with practices of circumvention. Interested parties other than directly affected or benefited parties, such as environmental organisations and non-

governmental organisations, which find concrete evidence of practices of circumvention may also notify the Commission.

5. The notification referred to in paragraph 4 shall state the reasons on which it is based and shall include relevant data and statistics to support the claim of circumvention of this Regulation. The Commission shall initiate an investigation into a claim of circumvention either where it has been notified by a Member State, or by an affected, benefited or other interested party, provided that the notification meets the requirements referred to in this paragraph, or where the Commission itself determines that such an investigation is necessary. In carrying out the investigation, the Commission may be assisted by the competent authorities and customs authorities. The Commission shall conclude the investigation within nine months from the date of notification. Where an investigation has been initiated, the Commission shall notify all competent authorities.

6. Where the Commission, taking into account the relevant data, reports and statistics, including those provided by customs authorities, has sufficient reasons to believe that the circumstances referred to in paragraph 2, point (a) of this Article, are occurring in one or more Member States by way of an established pattern, it is empowered to adopt delegated acts in accordance with Article 28 to amend the list of goods in Annex I by adding the relevant

slightly modified products referred to in paragraph 2, point (a), of this Article, for anti-circumvention purposes.

CHAPTER VII

EXERCISE OF THE DELEGATION AND COMMITTEE PROCEDURE

Article 28
Exercise of the delegation

1. The power to adopt delegated acts is conferred on the Commission subject to the conditions laid down in this Article.

2. The power to adopt delegated acts referred to in Articles 2(10), 2(11), 18(3), 20(6) and 27(6) shall be conferred on the Commission for a period of five years from 17 May 2023. The Commission shall draw up a report in respect of the delegation of power not later than nine months before the end of the five-year period. The delegation of power shall be tacitly extended for further periods of an identical duration, unless the European Parliament or the Council opposes such extension not later than three months before the end of each period.

3. The delegation of power referred to in Articles 2(10), 2(11), 18(3), 20(6) and 27(6) may be revoked at any time by the European

Parliament or by the Council.

4. A decision to revoke shall put an end to the delegation of the power specified in that decision. It shall take effect the day following the publication of the decision in the *Official Journal of the European Union* or at a later date specified therein. It shall not affect the validity of any delegated act already in force.

5. Before adopting a delegated act, the Commission shall consult experts designated by each Member State in accordance with the principles laid down in the Inter-institutional Agreement of 13 April 2016 on Better Law-Making.

6. As soon as it adopts a delegated act, the Commission shall notify it simultaneously to the European Parliament and to the Council.

7. A delegated act adopted pursuant to Articles 2(10), 2(11), 18(3), 20(6) or 27(6) shall enter into force only if no objection has been expressed either by the European Parliament or by the Council within a period of two months of notification of that act to the European Parliament and to the Council or if, before the expiry of that period, the European Parliament and the Council have both informed the Commission that they will not object. That period shall be extended by two months at the initiative of the European Parliament or of the Council.

Article 29

Committee procedure

1. The Commission shall be assisted by the CBAM Committee. That committee shall be a committee within the meaning of Regulation (EU) No 182/2011.

2. Where reference is made to this paragraph, Article 5 of Regulation (EU) No 182/2011 shall apply.

CHAPTER VIII

REPORTING AND REVIEW

Article 30
Review and reporting by the Commission

1. The Commission, in consultation with relevant stakeholders, shall collect the information necessary with a view to extending the scope of this Regulation as indicated in and pursuant to paragraph 2, point (a), and to developing methods of calculating embedded emissions based on environmental footprint methods.

2. Before the end of the transitional period referred to in Article 32, the Commission shall present a report to the European Parliament and to the Council on the application of this Regulation.

   The report shall contain an assessment of:

   (a) the possibility to extend the scope to:

   (i) embedded indirect emissions in the goods listed in Annex II;

   (ii) embedded emissions in the transport of the goods listed in Annex I and transportation services;

   (iii) goods at risk of carbon leakage other than those listed in Annex I, and specifically organic chemicals and polymers;

   (iv) other input materials (precursors) for the goods listed in

Annex I;

(b) the criteria to be used to identify goods to be included in the list in Annex I to this Regulation based on the sectors at risk of carbon leakage identified pursuant to Article 10b of Directive 2003/87/EC; that assessment shall be accompanied by a timetable ending in 2030 for the gradual inclusion of the goods within the scope of this Regulation, taking into account in particular the level of risk of their respective carbon leakage;

(c) the technical requirements for calculating embedded emissions for other goods to be included in the list in Annex I;

(d) the progress made in international discussions regarding climate action;

(e) the governance system, including the administrative costs;

(f) the impact of this Regulation on goods listed in Annex I imported from developing countries with special interest to the least developed countries as identified by the United Nations (LDCs) and on the effects of the technical assistance given;

(g) the methodology for the calculation of indirect emissions pursuant to Article 7(7) and point 4.3 of Annex IV.

3. At least one year before the end of the transitional period, the Commission shall present a report to the European Parliament and to the Council that identifies products further down the value chain of the goods listed in Annex I that it recommends to be

considered for inclusion within the scope of this Regulation. To that end, the Commission shall develop, in a timely manner, a methodology that should be based on relevance in terms of cumulated greenhouse gas emissions and risk of carbon leakage.

4. The reports referred to in paragraphs 2 and 3 shall, where appropriate, be accompanied by a legislative proposal by the end of the transitional period, including a detailed impact assessment, in particular with a view to extending the scope of this Regulation on the basis of the conclusions drawn in those reports.

5. Every two years from the end of the transitional period, as part of its annual report to the European Parliament and to the Council pursuant to Article 10(5) of Directive 2003/87/EC, the Commission shall assess the effectiveness of the CBAM in addressing the carbon leakage risk of goods produced in the Union for export to third countries which do not apply the EU ETS or a similar carbon pricing mechanism. The report shall in particular assess the development of Union exports in CBAM sectors and the developments as regards trade flows and the embedded emissions of those goods on the global market. Where the report concludes that there is a risk of carbon leakage of goods produced in the Union for export to such third countries which do not apply the EU ETS or a similar carbon pricing mechanism, the Commission shall, where appropriate, present a legislative proposal to address

that risk in a manner that complies with World Trade Organization law and that takes into account the decarbonisation of installations in the Union.

6. The Commission shall monitor the functioning of the CBAM with a view to evaluating the impacts and possible adjustments in its application.

Before 1 January 2028, as well as every two years thereafter, the Commission shall present a report to the European Parliament and to the Council on the application of this Regulation and functioning of the CBAM. The report shall contain at least the following:

(a) an assessment of the impact of the CBAM on:

    (i) carbon leakage, including in relation to exports;

    (ii) the sectors covered;

    (iii) internal market, economic and territorial impact throughout the Union;

    (iv) inflation and the price of commodities;

    (v) the effect on industries using goods listed in Annex I;

    (vi) international trade, including resource shuffling; and

    (vii) LDCs;

(b) an assessment of:

    (i) the governance system, including an assessment of the implementation and administration of the authorisation of

CBAM declarants by Member States;

(ii) the scope of this Regulation;

(iii) practices of circumvention;

(iv) the application of penalties in Member States;

(c) results of investigations and penalties imposed;

(d) aggregated information on the emission intensity for each country of origin for the different goods listed in Annex I.

7. Where an unforeseeable, exceptional and unprovoked event has occurred that is outside the control of one or more third countries subject to the CBAM, and that event has destructive consequences on the economic and industrial infrastructure of such country or countries concerned, the Commission shall assess the situation and submit to the European Parliament and to the Council a report, accompanied, where appropriate, by a legislative proposal, to amend this Regulation by setting out the necessary provisional measures to address those exceptional circumstances.

8. From the end of the transitional period referred to in Article 32 of this Regulation, as part of the annual reporting pursuant to Article 41 of Regulation (EU) 2021/947 of the European Parliament and of the Council ([6]), the Commission shall evaluate

---

6 Regulation (EU) 2021/947 of the European Parliament and of the Council of 9 June 2021 establishing the Neighbourhood, Development and International Cooperation Instrument – Global Europe, amending and

and report on how the financing under that Regulation has contributed to the decarbonisation of the manufacturing industry in LDCs.

---

repealing Decision No 466/2014/EU of the European Parliament and of the Council and repealing Regulation (EU) 2017/1601 of the European Parliament and of the Council and Council Regulation (EC, Euratom) No 480/2009 (OJ L 209, 14.6.2021, p. 1).

CHAPTER IX

COORDINATION WITH FREE ALLOCATION OF ALLOWANCES UNDER THE EU ETS

Article 31

Free allocation of allowances under the EU ETS and obligation to surrender CBAM certificates

1. The CBAM certificates to be surrendered in accordance with Article 22 of this Regulation shall be adjusted to reflect the extent to which EU ETS allowances are allocated free of charge in accordance with Article 10a of Directive 2003/87/EC to installations producing, within the Union, the goods listed in Annex I to this Regulation.

2. The Commission is empowered to adopt implementing acts laying down detailed rules for the calculation of the adjustment as referred to in paragraph 1 of this Article. Such detailed rules shall be elaborated by reference to the principles applied in the EU ETS for the free allocation of allowances to installations producing, within the Union, the goods listed in Annex I, taking account of the different benchmarks used in the EU ETS for free allocation with a view to combining those benchmarks into corresponding

values for the goods concerned, and taking into account relevant input materials (precursors). Those implementing acts shall be adopted in accordance with the examination procedure referred to in Article 29(2).

CHAPTER X

TRANSITIONAL PROVISIONS

Article 32
Scope of the transitional period

During the transitional period from 1 October 2023 until 31 December 2025, the obligations of the importer under this Regulation shall be limited to the reporting obligations set out in Articles 33, 34 and 35 of this Regulation. Where the importer is established in a Member State and appoints an indirect customs representative in accordance with Article 18 of Regulation (EU) No 952/2013, and where the indirect customs representative so agrees, the reporting obligations shall apply to such indirect customs representative. Where the importer is not established in a Member State, the reporting obligations shall apply to the indirect customs representative.

Article 33
Importation of goods

1. The customs authorities shall inform the importer or, in the situations covered by Article 32, the indirect customs

representative of the reporting obligation referred to in Article 35 no later than at the moment of the release of goods for free circulation.

2. The customs authorities shall periodically and automatically, in particular by means of the surveillance mechanism established pursuant to Article 56(5) of Regulation (EU) No 952/2013 or by electronic means of data transmission, communicate to the Commission information on imported goods, including processed products resulting from the outward processing procedure. Such information shall include the EORI number of the customs declarant and of the importer, the eight-digit CN code, the quantity, the country of origin, the date of the customs declaration and the customs procedure.

3. The Commission shall communicate the information referred to in paragraph 2 to the competent authorities of the Member States where the customs declarant and, where applicable, the importer are established.

Article 34
Reporting obligation for certain customs procedures

1. Where processed products resulting from the inward processing procedure as referred to in Article 256 of Regulation (EU)

No 952/2013 are imported, the reporting obligation referred to in Article 35 of this Regulation shall include the information on the goods that were placed under the inward processing procedure and resulted in the imported processed products, even if the processed products are not listed in Annex I to this Regulation. This paragraph shall also apply where the processed products resulting from the inward processing procedure are returned goods as referred to in Article 205 of Regulation (EU) No 952/2013.

2. The reporting obligation referred to in Article 35 of this Regulation shall not apply to the import of:

(a) processed products resulting from the outward processing procedure as referred to in Article 259 of Regulation (EU) No 952/2013;

(b) goods qualifying as returned goods in accordance with Article 203 of Regulation (EU) No 952/2013.

Article 35
Reporting obligation

1. Each importer or, in the situations covered by Article 32, the indirect customs representative, having imported goods during a given quarter of a calendar year shall, for that quarter, submit a report ('CBAM report') containing information on the goods

imported during that quarter, to the Commission, no later than one month after the end of that quarter.

2. The CBAM report shall include the following information:

(a) the total quantity of each type of goods, expressed in megawatt-hours for electricity and in tonnes for other goods, specified for each installation producing the goods in the country of origin;

(b) the actual total embedded emissions, expressed in tonnes of CO_2e emissions per megawatt-hour of electricity or for other goods in tonnes of CO_2e emissions per tonne of each type of goods, calculated in accordance with the method set out in Annex IV;

(c) the total indirect emissions calculated in accordance with the implementing act referred to in paragraph 7;

(d) the carbon price due in a country of origin for the embedded emissions in the imported goods, taking into account any rebate or other form of compensation available.

3. The Commission shall periodically communicate to the relevant competent authorities a list of those importers or indirect customs representatives established in the Member State, including the corresponding justifications, which it has reasons to believe have failed to comply with the obligation to submit a CBAM report in accordance with paragraph 1.

4. Where the Commission considers that a CBAM report is

incomplete or incorrect, it shall communicate to the competent authority of the Member State where the importer is established or, in the situations covered by Article 32, the indirect customs representative is established, the additional information it considers necessary to complete or correct that report. Such information shall be provided for indicative purposes and without prejudice to the definitive appreciation by that competent authority. That competent authority shall initiate the correction procedure and notify the importer or, in the situations covered by Article 32, the indirect customs representative of the additional information necessary to correct that report. Where appropriate, that importer or that indirect customs representative shall submit a corrected report to the competent authority concerned and to the Commission.

5. Where the competent authority of the Member State referred to in paragraph 4 of this Article initiates a correction procedure, including in consideration of information received in accordance with paragraph 4 of this Article, and determines that the importer or, where applicable in accordance with Article 32, the indirect customs representative has not taken the necessary steps to correct the CBAM report, or where the competent authority concerned determines, including in consideration of information received in accordance with paragraph 3 of this Article, that the importer or,

where applicable in accordance with Article 32, the indirect customs representative has failed to comply with the obligation to submit a CBAM report in accordance with paragraph 1 of this Article, that competent authority shall impose an effective, proportionate and dissuasive penalty on the importer or, where applicable in accordance with Article 32, the indirect customs representative. To that end, the competent authority shall notify the importer or, where applicable in accordance with Article 32, the indirect customs representative and inform the Commission, of the following:

(a) the conclusion, and reasons for that conclusion, that the importer or, where applicable in accordance with Article 32, the indirect customs representative has failed to comply with the obligation of submitting a report for a given quarter or to take the necessary steps to correct the report;

(b) the amount of the penalty imposed on the importer or, where applicable in accordance with Article 32, the indirect customs representative;

(c) the date from which the penalty is due;

(d) the action that the importer or, where applicable in accordance with Article 32, the indirect customs representative is to take to pay the penalty; and

(e) the right of the importer or, where applicable in accordance with Article 32, the indirect customs representative to appeal.

6. Where the competent authority, after receiving the information from the Commission under this Article, decides not to take any action, the competent authority shall inform the Commission accordingly.

7. The Commission is empowered to adopt implementing acts concerning:

(a) the information to be reported, the means and format for that reporting, including detailed information per country of origin and type of goods to support the totals referred to in paragraph 2, points (a), (b) and (c), and examples of any relevant rebate or other form of compensation available as referred to in paragraph 2, point (d);

(b) the indicative range of penalties to be imposed pursuant to paragraph 5 and the criteria to take into account for determining the actual amount, including the gravity and duration of the failure to report;

(c) detailed rules on the conversion of the yearly average carbon price due referred to in paragraph 2, point (d), expressed in foreign currency into euro at the yearly average exchange rate;

(d) detailed rules on the elements of the calculation methods set out in Annex IV, including determining system boundaries of production processes, emission factors, installation-specific values of actual emissions and their respective application to individual goods as well as laying down methods to ensure the reliability of data, including the level of detail; and

(e) the means and format for the reporting requirements for indirect emissions in imported goods; that format shall include the quantity of electricity used for the production of the goods listed in Annex I, as well as the country of origin, generation source and emission factors related to that electricity.

Those implementing acts shall be adopted in accordance with the examination procedure referred to in Article 29(2) of this Regulation. They shall apply for goods imported during the transitional period referred to in Article 32 of this Regulation and shall build upon existing legislation for installations that fall within the scope of Directive 2003/87/EC.

CHAPTER XI

FINAL PROVISIONS

Article 36

Entry into force

1. This Regulation shall enter into force on the day following that of its publication in the *Official Journal of the European Union*.

2. It shall apply from 1 October 2023. However:

    (a) Articles 5, 10, 14, 16 and 17 shall apply from 31 December 2024;

    (b) Article 2(2) and Articles 4, 6 to 9, 15 and 19, Article 20(1), (3), (4) and (5), Articles 21 to 27 and 31 shall apply from 1 January 2026.

This Regulation shall be binding in its entirety and directly applicable in all Member States.

Done at Strasbourg, 10 May 2023.

For the European Parliament

The President

R. METSOLA

For the Council

The President

J. ROSWALL

List of goods and greenhouse gases

1. For the purpose of the identification of goods, this Regulation shall apply to goods falling under the Combined Nomenclature ('CN') codes set out in the following table. The CN codes shall be those under Regulation (EEC) No 2658/87.

2. For the purposes of this Regulation, the greenhouse gases relating to goods referred to in point 1, shall be those set out in the following table for the goods concerned.

Cement

CN code	Greenhouse gas
2507 00 80 – Other kaolinic clays	Carbon dioxide
2523 10 00 – Cement clinkers	Carbon dioxide
2523 21 00 – White Portland cement, whether or not artificially coloured	Carbon dioxide
2523 29 00 – Other Portland cement	Carbon dioxide
2523 30 00 – Aluminous cement	Carbon dioxide
2523 90 00 – Other hydraulic cements	Carbon dioxide

Electricity

CN code	Greenhouse gas
2716 00 00 – Electrical energy	Carbon dioxide

Fertilisers

CN code	Greenhouse gas
2808 00 00 – Nitric acid; sulphonitric acids	Carbon dioxide and nitrous oxide
2814 – Ammonia, anhydrous or in aqueous solution	Carbon dioxide
2834 21 00 – Nitrates of potassium	Carbon dioxide and nitrous oxide
3102 – Mineral or chemical fertilisers, nitrogenous	Carbon dioxide and nitrous oxide
3105 – Mineral or chemical fertilisers containing two or three of the fertilising elements nitrogen, phosphorus and potassium; other fertilisers; goods of this chapter in tablets or similar forms or in packages of a gross weight not exceeding 10 kg Except: 3105 60 00 – Mineral or chemical fertilisers containing the two fertilising elements phosphorus and potassium	Carbon dioxide and nitrous oxide

歐盟CBAM法規：台灣廠商因應之道與申報準備

Iron and steel

CN code	Greenhouse gas
72 – Iron and steel Except: 7202 2 – Ferro-silicon 7202 30 00 – Ferro-silico-manganese 7202 50 00 – Ferro-silico-chromium 7202 70 00 – Ferro-molybdenum 7202 80 00–Ferro-tungsten and ferro-silico-tungsten 7202 91 00–Ferro-titanium and ferro-silico-titanium 7202 92 00 – Ferro-vanadium 7202 93 00 – Ferro-niobium 7202 99 – Other: 7202 99 10 – Ferro-phosphorus 7202 99 30 – Ferro-silico-magnesium 7202 99 80 – Other 7204 – Ferrous waste and scrap; remelting scrap ingots and steel	Carbon dioxide
2601 12 00 – Agglomerated iron ores and concentrates, other than roasted iron pyrites	Carbon dioxide
7301 – Sheet piling of iron or steel, whether or not drilled, punched or made from assembled elements; welded angles, shapes and sections, of iron or steel	Carbon dioxide
7302 – Railway or tramway track construction material of iron or steel, the following: rails, check-rails and rack rails, switch blades, crossing frogs, point rods and other crossing pieces, sleepers (cross-ties), fish- plates, chairs, chair wedges, sole plates (base plates), rail clips, bedplates, ties and other material specialised for jointing or fixing rails	Carbon dioxide
7303 00 – Tubes, pipes and hollow profiles, of cast iron	Carbon dioxide
7304 – Tubes, pipes and hollow profiles, seamless, of iron (other than cast iron) or steel	Carbon dioxide

CN code	Greenhouse gas
7305 – Other tubes and pipes (for example, welded, riveted or similarly closed), having circular cross-sections, the external diameter of which exceeds 406,4 mm, of iron or steel	Carbon dioxide
7306 – Other tubes, pipes and hollow profiles (for example, open seam or welded, riveted or similarly closed), of iron or steel	Carbon dioxide
7307 – Tube or pipe fittings (for example, couplings, elbows, sleeves), of iron or steel	Carbon dioxide
7308 – Structures (excluding prefabricated buildings of heading 9406) and parts of structures (for example, bridges and bridge-sections, lock- gates, towers, lattice masts, roofs, roofing frameworks, doors and windows and their frames and thresholds for doors, shutters, balustrades, pillars and columns), of iron or steel; plates, rods, angles, shapes, sections, tubes and the like, prepared for use in structures, of iron or steel	Carbon dioxide
7309 00 – Reservoirs, tanks, vats and similar containers for any material (other than compressed or liquefied gas), of iron or steel, of a capacity exceeding 300 l, whether or not lined or heat-insulated, but not fitted with mechanical or thermal equipment	Carbon dioxide
7310 – Tanks, casks, drums, cans, boxes and similar containers, for any material (other than compressed or liquefied gas), of iron or steel, of a capacity not exceeding 300 l, whether or not lined or heat-insulated, but not fitted with mechanical or thermal equipment	Carbon dioxide
7311 00 – Containers for compressed or liquefied gas, of iron or steel	Carbon dioxide
7318 – Screws, bolts, nuts, coach screws, screw hooks, rivets, cotters, cotter pins, washers (including spring washers) and similar articles, of iron or steel	Carbon dioxide

歐盟CBAM法規：台灣廠商因應之道與申報準備

CN code	Greenhouse gas
7326 – Other articles of iron or steel	Carbon dioxide

Aluminium

CN code	Greenhouse gas
7601 – Unwrought aluminium	Carbon dioxide and perfluorocarbons
7603 – Aluminium powders and flakes	Carbon dioxide and perfluorocarbons
7604 – Aluminium bars, rods and profiles	Carbon dioxide and perfluorocarbons
7605 – Aluminium wire	Carbon dioxide and perfluorocarbons
7606 – Aluminium plates, sheets and strip, of a thickness exceeding 0,2 mm	Carbon dioxide and perfluorocarbons
7607 – Aluminium foil (whether or not printed or backed with paper, paper-board, plastics or similar backing materials) of a thickness (excluding any backing) not exceeding 0,2 mm	Carbon dioxide and perfluorocarbons
7608 – Aluminium tubes and pipes	Carbon dioxide and perfluorocarbons
7609 00 00 – Aluminium tube or pipe fittings (for example, couplings, elbows, sleeves)	Carbon dioxide and perfluorocarbons
7610 – Aluminium structures (excluding prefabricated buildings of heading 9406) and parts of structures (for example, bridges and bridge-sections, towers, lattice masts, roofs, roofing frameworks, doors and windows and their frames and thresholds for doors, balustrades, pillars and columns); aluminium plates, rods, profiles, tubes and the like, prepared for use in structures	Carbon dioxide and perfluorocarbons

CN code	Greenhouse gas
7611 00 00 – Aluminium reservoirs, tanks, vats and similar containers, for any material (other than compressed or liquefied gas), of a capacity exceeding 300 litres, whether or not lined or heat-insulated, but not fitted with mechanical or thermal equipment	Carbon dioxide and perfluorocarbons
7612 – Aluminium casks, drums, cans, boxes and similar containers (including rigid or collapsible tubular containers), for any material (other than compressed or liquefied gas), of a capacity not exceeding 300 litres, whether or not lined or heat-insulated, but not fitted with mechanical or thermal equipment	Carbon dioxide and perfluorocarbons
7613 00 00 – Aluminium containers for compressed or liquefied gas	Carbon dioxide and perfluorocarbons
7614 – Stranded wire, cables, plaited bands and the like, of aluminium, not electrically insulated	Carbon dioxide and perfluorocarbons
7616 – Other articles of aluminium	Carbon dioxide and perfluorocarbons

Chemicals

CN code	Greenhouse gas
2804 10 00 – Hydrogen	Carbon dioxide

歐盟CBAM法規：台灣廠商因應之道與申報準備

List of goods for which only direct emissions are to be taken into account, pursuant to Article 7(1)

Iron and steel

CN code	Greenhouse gas
72 – Iron and steel Except: 7202 2 – Ferro-silicon 7202 30 00 – Ferro-silico-manganese 7202 50 00 – Ferro-silico-chromium 7202 70 00 – Ferro-molybdenum 7202 80 00 – Ferro-tungsten and ferro-silico-tungsten 7202 91 00 – Ferro-titanium and ferro-silico-titanium 7202 92 00 – Ferro-vanadium 7202 93 00 – Ferro-niobium 7202 99 – Other: 7202 99 10 – Ferro-phosphorus 7202 99 30 – Ferro-silico-magnesium 7202 99 80 – Other 7204 – Ferrous waste and scrap; remelting scrap ingots and steel	Carbon dioxide
7301 – Sheet piling of iron or steel, whether or not drilled, punched or made from assembled elements; welded angles, shapes and sections, of iron or steel	Carbon dioxide

CN code	Greenhouse gas
7302 – Railway or tramway track construction material of iron or steel, the following: rails, check-rails and rack rails, switch blades, crossing frogs, point rods and other crossing pieces, sleepers (cross-ties), fish- plates, chairs, chair wedges, sole plates (base plates), rail clips, bedplates, ties and other material specialised for jointing or fixing rails	Carbon dioxide
7303 00 – Tubes, pipes and hollow profiles, of cast iron	Carbon dioxide
7304 – Tubes, pipes and hollow profiles, seamless, of iron (other than cast iron) or steel	Carbon dioxide
7305 – Other tubes and pipes (for example, welded, riveted or similarly closed), having circular cross-sections, the external diameter of which exceeds 406,4 mm, of iron or steel	Carbon dioxide
7306 – Other tubes, pipes and hollow profiles (for example, open seam or welded, riveted or similarly closed), of iron or steel	Carbon dioxide
7307 – Tube or pipe fittings (for example, couplings, elbows, sleeves), of iron or steel	Carbon dioxide
7308 – Structures (excluding prefabricated buildings of heading 9406) and parts of structures (for example, bridges and bridge-sections, lock- gates, towers, lattice masts, roofs, roofing frameworks, doors and windows and their frames and thresholds for doors, shutters, balustrades, pillars and columns), of iron or steel; plates, rods, angles, shapes, sections, tubes and the like, prepared for use in structures, of iron or steel	Carbon dioxide
7309 00 – Reservoirs, tanks, vats and similar containers for any material (other than compressed or liquefied gas), of iron or steel, of a capacity exceeding 300 l, whether or not lined or heat-insulated, but not fitted with mechanical or thermal equipment	Carbon dioxide

歐盟CBAM法規：台灣廠商因應之道與申報準備

CN code	Greenhouse gas
7310 – Tanks, casks, drums, cans, boxes and similar containers, for any material (other than compressed or liquefied gas), of iron or steel, of a capacity not exceeding 300 l, whether or not lined or heat-insulated, but not fitted with mechanical or thermal equipment	Carbon dioxide
7311 00 – Containers for compressed or liquefied gas, of iron or steel	Carbon dioxide
7318 – Screws, bolts, nuts, coach screws, screw hooks, rivets, cotters, cotter pins, washers (including spring washers) and similar articles, of iron or steel	Carbon dioxide
7326 – Other articles of iron or steel	Carbon dioxide

Aluminium

CN code	Greenhouse gas
7601 – Unwrought aluminium	Carbon dioxide and perfluorocarbons
7603 – Aluminium powders and flakes	Carbon dioxide and perfluorocarbons
7604 – Aluminium bars, rods and profiles	Carbon dioxide and perfluorocarbons
7605 – Aluminium wire	Carbon dioxide and perfluorocarbons
7606 – Aluminium plates, sheets and strip, of a thickness exceeding 0,2 mm	Carbon dioxide and perfluorocarbons
7607 – Aluminium foil (whether or not printed or backed with paper, paper-board, plastics or similar backing materials) of a thickness (excluding any backing) not exceeding 0,2 mm	Carbon dioxide and perfluorocarbons
7608 – Aluminium tubes and pipes	Carbon dioxide and perfluorocarbons

CN code	Greenhouse gas
7609 00 00 – Aluminium tube or pipe fittings (for example, couplings, elbows, sleeves)	Carbon dioxide and perfluorocarbons
7610 – Aluminium structures (excluding prefabricated buildings of heading 9406) and parts of structures (for example, bridges and bridge-sections, towers, lattice masts, roofs, roofing frameworks, doors and windows and their frames and thresholds for doors, balustrades, pillars and columns); aluminium plates, rods, profiles, tubes and the like, prepared for use in structures	Carbon dioxide and perfluorocarbons
7611 00 00 – Aluminium reservoirs, tanks, vats and similar containers, for any material (other than compressed or liquefied gas), of a capacity exceeding 300 litres, whether or not lined or heat-insulated, but not fitted with mechanical or thermal equipment	Carbon dioxide and perfluorocarbons
7612 – Aluminium casks, drums, cans, boxes and similar containers (including rigid or collapsible tubular containers), for any material (other than compressed or liquefied gas), of a capacity not exceeding 300 litres, whether or not lined or heat-insulated, but not fitted with mechanical or thermal equipment	Carbon dioxide and perfluorocarbons
7613 00 00 – Aluminium containers for compressed or liquefied gas	Carbon dioxide and perfluorocarbons
7614 – Stranded wire, cables, plaited bands and the like, of aluminium, not electrically insulated	Carbon dioxide and perfluorocarbons
7616 – Other articles of aluminium	Carbon dioxide and perfluorocarbons

Chemicals

CN code	Greenhouse gas
2804 10 00 – Hydrogen	Carbon dioxide

Third countries and territories outside the scope of this Regulation for the purpose of Article 2

1. THIRD COUNTRIES AND TERRITORIES OUTSIDE THE SCOPE OF THIS REGULATION

This Regulation shall not apply to goods originating in the following countries:

— Iceland

— Liechtenstein

— Norway

— Switzerland

This Regulation shall not apply to goods originating in the following territories:

— Büsingen

— Heligoland

— Livigno

— Ceuta

— Melilla

2. THIRD COUNTRIES AND TERRITORIES OUTSIDE THE SCOPE OF THIS REGULATION WITH REGARD TO THE IMPORTATION OF ELECTRICITY INTO THE CUSTOMS TERRITORY OF THE UNION

[Third countries or territories to be added or removed by the Commission pursuant to Article 2(11).]

Methods for calculating embedded emissions for the purpose of Article 7

1. DEFINITIONS

For the purposes of this Annex and of Annexes V and VI, the following definitions apply:

(a) 'simple goods' means goods produced in a production process requiring exclusively input materials (precursors) and fuels having zero embedded emissions;

(b) 'complex goods' means goods other than simple goods;

(c) 'specific embedded emissions' means the embedded emissions of one tonne of goods, expressed as tonnes of CO_2e emissions per tonne of goods;

(d) 'CO_2 emission factor', means the weighted average of the CO_2 intensity of electricity produced from fossil fuels within a geographic area; the CO_2 emission factor is the result of the division of the CO_2 emission data of the electricity sector by the gross electricity generation based on fossil fuels in the relevant geographic area; it is expressed in tonnes of CO_2 per megawatt-hour;

(e) 'emission factor for electricity' means the default value, expressed in CO_2e, representing the emission intensity of electricity consumed in production of goods;

(f) 'power purchase agreement' means a contract under which a person agrees to purchase electricity directly from an electricity producer;

(g) 'transmission system operator' means an operator as defined in Article 2, point (35), of Directive (EU) 2019/944 of the European Parliament and of the Council ([7]).

2. DETERMINATION OF ACTUAL SPECIFIC EMBEDDED EMISSIONS FOR SIMPLE GOODS

For determining the specific actual embedded emissions of simple goods produced in a given installation, direct and, where applicable, indirect emissions shall be accounted for. For that purpose, the following equation is to be applied:

$$SEE_g = \frac{AttrEm_g}{AL_g}$$

Where:

SEE_g are the specific embedded emissions of goods g, in terms of CO_2e per tonne;

$AttrEm_g$ are the attributed emissions of goods g, and

---

7 Directive (EU) 2019/944 of the European Parliament and of the Council of 5 June 2019 on common rules for the internal market for electricity and amending Directive 2012/27/EU (OJ L 158, 14.6.2019, p. 125).

AL_g is the activity level of the goods, being the quantity of the goods produced in the reporting period in that installation.

'Attributed emissions' mean the part of the installation's emissions during the reporting period that are caused by the production process resulting in goods g when applying the system boundaries of the production process defined by the implementing acts adopted pursuant to Article 7(7). The attributed emissions shall be calculated using the following equation:

$$AttrEm_g = DirEm + IndirEm$$

Where:

DirEm are the direct emissions, resulting from the production process, expressed in tonnes of CO_2e, within the system boundaries referred to in the implementing act adopted pursuant to Article 7(7), and

IndirEm are the indirect emissions resulting from the production of electricity consumed in the production processes of goods, expressed in tonnes of CO_2e, within the system boundaries referred to in the implementing act adopted pursuant to Article 7(7).

3. DETERMINATION OF ACTUAL EMBEDDED EMISSIONS FOR COMPLEX GOODS

For determining the specific actual embedded emissions of complex goods produced in a given installation, the following equation is to be applied:

$$SEE_g = \frac{AttrEm_g + EE_{InpMat}}{AL_g}$$

Where:

$AttrEm_g$ are the attributed emissions of goods g;

AL_g is the activity level of the goods, being the quantity of goods produced in the reporting period in that installation, and

EE_{InpMat} are the embedded emissions of the input materials (precursors) consumed in the production process. Only input materials (precursors) listed as relevant to the system boundaries of the production process as specified in the implementing act adopted pursuant to Article 7(7) are to be considered. The relevant EE_{InpMat} are calculated as follows:

$$EE_{InpMat} = \sum_{i=1}^{n} M_i \cdot SEE_i$$

Where:

M_i is the mass of input material (precursor) i used in the production process, and

SEE_i are the specific embedded emissions for the input material (precursor) i. For SEE_i the operator of the installation shall use the value of emissions resulting from the installation where the input material (precursor) was produced, provided that that installation's data can be adequately measured.

4. DETERMINATION OF DEFAULT VALUES REFERRED TO IN ARTICLE 7(2) AND (3)

For the purpose of determining default values, only actual values shall be used for the determination of embedded emissions. In the absence of actual data, literature values may be used. The Commission shall publish guidance for the approach taken to correct for waste gases or greenhouse gases used as process input, before collecting the data required to determine the relevant default values for each type of goods listed in Annex I. Default values shall be determined based on the best available data. Best available data shall be based on reliable and publicly available information. Default values shall be revised periodically through the implementing acts adopted pursuant to Article 7(7) based on the most up-to-date and reliable information, including on the basis of information provided by a third country or group of third countries.

歐盟CBAM法規：台灣廠商因應之道與申報準備

4.1. Default values referred to in Article 7(2)

When actual emissions cannot be adequately determined by the authorised CBAM declarant, default values shall be used. Those values shall be set at the average emission intensity of each exporting country and for each of the goods listed in Annex I other than electricity, increased by a proportionately designed mark-up. This mark-up shall be determined in the implementing acts adopted pursuant to Article 7(7) and shall be set at an appropriate level to ensure the environmental integrity of the CBAM, building on the most up-to-date and reliable information, including on the basis of information gathered during the transitional period. When reliable data for the exporting country cannot be applied for a type of goods, the default values shall be based on the average emission intensity of the X % worst performing EU ETS installations for that type of goods. The value of X shall be determined in the implementing acts adopted pursuant to Article 7(7) and shall be set at an appropriate level to ensure the environmental integrity of the CBAM, building on the most up-to-date and reliable information, including on the basis of information gathered during the transitional period.

4.2. Default values for imported electricity referred to in Article 7(3)

Default values for imported electricity shall be determined for a third country, group of third countries or region within a third country based on either specific default values, in accordance with point 4.2.1, or, if those values are not available, on alternative default values, in accordance with point 4.2.2.

Where the electricity is produced in a third country, group of third countries or region within a third country, and transits through third countries, groups of third countries, regions within a third country or Member States with the purpose of being imported into the Union, the default values to be used are those from the third country, group of third countries or region within a third country where the electricity was produced.

4.2.1. Specific default values for a third country, group of third countries or region within a third country

Specific default values shall be set at the CO_2 emission factor in the third country, group of third countries or region within a third country, based on the best data available to the Commission.

4.2.2. Alternative default values

Where a specific default value is not available for a third country, a group of third countries, or a region within a third country, the alternative default value for electricity shall be set at the CO_2 emission factor in the Union.

Where it can be demonstrated, on the basis of reliable data, that the CO_2 emission factor in a third country, a group of third countries or a region within a third country is lower than the specific default value determined by the Commission or lower than the CO_2 emission factor in the Union, an alternative default value based on that CO_2 emission factor may be used for that third country, group of third countries or region within a third country.

4.3. Default values for embedded indirect emissions

Default values for the indirect emissions embedded in a good produced in a third country shall be determined on a default value calculated on the average, of either the emission factor of the Union electricity grid, the emission factor of the country of origin electricity grid or the CO_2 emission factor of price-setting sources in the country of origin, of the electricity used for the production of that good.

Where a third country, or a group of third countries, demonstrates to the Commission, on the basis of reliable data, that the average electricity mix emission factor or CO_2 emission factor of price-setting sources in the third country or group of third countries is lower than the default value for indirect emissions, an alternative default value based on that average CO_2 emission factor shall be established for this country or group of countries.

The Commission shall adopt, no later than 30 June 2025, an implementing act pursuant to Article 7(7) to further specify which of the calculation methods determined in accordance with the first subparagraph shall apply to the calculation of default values. For that purpose, the Commission shall base itself on the most up-to-date and reliable data, including on data gathered during the transitional period, as regards the quantity of electricity used for the production of the goods listed in Annex I, as well as the country of origin, generation source and emission factors related to that electricity. The specific calculation method shall be determined on the basis of the most appropriate way to achieve both of the following criteria:

— the prevention of carbon leakage;

— ensuring the environmental integrity of the CBAM.

5. CONDITIONS FOR APPLYING ACTUAL EMBEDDED EMISSIONS IN IMPORTED ELECTRICITY

An authorised CBAM declarant may apply actual embedded emissions instead of default values for the calculation referred to in

歐盟CBAM法規：台灣廠商因應之道與申報準備

Article 7(3) if the following cumulative criteria are met:

(a) the amount of electricity for which the use of actual embedded emissions is claimed is covered by a power purchase agreement between the authorised CBAM declarant and a producer of electricity located in a third country;

(b) the installation producing electricity is either directly connected to the Union transmission system or it can be demonstrated that at the time of export there was no physical network congestion at any point in the network between the installation and the Union transmission system;

(c) the installation producing electricity does not emit more than 550 grammes of CO_2 of fossil fuel origin per kilowatt-hour of electricity;

(d) the amount of electricity for which the use of actual embedded emissions is claimed has been firmly nominated to the allocated interconnection capacity by all responsible transmission system operators in the country of origin, the country of destination and, if relevant, each country of transit, and the nominated capacity and the production of electricity by the installation refer to the same period of time, which shall not be longer than one hour;

(e) the fulfilment of the above criteria is certified by an accredited verifier, who shall receive at least monthly interim reports demonstrating how those criteria are fulfilled.

The accumulated amount of electricity under the power purchase agreement and its corresponding actual embedded emissions shall be excluded from the calculation of the country emission factor or the CO_2 emission factor used for the purpose of the calculation of indirect electricity embedded emissions in goods in accordance with point 4.3, respectively.

6. CONDITIONS TO APPLYING ACTUAL EMBEDDED EMISSIONS FOR INDIRECT EMISSIONS

An authorised CBAM declarant may apply actual embedded emissions instead of default values for the calculation referred to in Article 7(4) if it can demonstrate a direct technical link between the installation in which the imported good is produced and the electricity generation source or if the operator of that installation has concluded a power purchase agreement with a producer of electricity located in a third country for an amount of electricity that is equivalent to the amount for which the use of a specific value is claimed.

7. ADAPTATION OF DEFAULT VALUES REFERRED TO IN ARTICLE 7(2) BASED ON REGION-SPECIFIC FEATURES

Default values can be adapted to particular areas and regions within third countries where specific characteristics prevail in terms of objective emission factors. When data adapted to those specific local characteristics are available and more targeted default values can be determined, the latter may be used.

Where declarants for goods originating in a third country, a group of third countries or a region within a third country can demonstrate, on the basis of reliable data, that alternative region-specific adaptations of default values are lower than the default values determined by the Commission, such region-specific adaptations can be used.

Bookkeeping requirements for information used for the calculation of embedded emissions for the purpose of Article 7(5)

1. MINIMUM DATA TO BE KEPT BY AN AUTHORISED CBAM DECLARANT FOR IMPORTED GOODS:

   1. Data identifying the authorised CBAM declarant:

      (a) name;

      (b) CBAM account number.

   2. Data on imported goods:

      (a) type and quantity of each type of goods;

      (b) country of origin;

      (c) actual emissions or default values.

2. MINIMUM DATA TO BE KEPT BY AN AUTHORISED CBAM DECLARANT FOR EMBEDDED EMISSIONS IN IMPORTED GOODS THAT ARE DETERMINED BASED ON ACTUAL EMISSIONS

   For each type of imported goods where embedded emissions are determined based on actual emissions, the following additional data shall be kept:

(a) identification of the installation where the goods were produced;

(b) contact information of the operator of the installation where the goods were produced;

(c) the verification reports as set out in Annex VI;

(d) the specific embedded emissions of the goods.

Verification principles and content of verification reports for the purpose of Article 8

1. PRINCIPLES OF VERIFICATION

The following principles shall apply:

(a) verifiers shall carry out verifications with an attitude of professional scepticism;

(b) the total embedded emissions to be declared in the CBAM declaration shall be considered as verified only if the verifier finds with reasonable assurance that the verification report is free of material misstatements and of material non-conformities regarding the calculation of embedded emissions in accordance with the rules of Annex IV;

(c) installation visits by the verifier shall be mandatory except where specific criteria for waiving the installation visit are met;

(d) for deciding whether misstatements or non-conformities are material, the verifier shall use thresholds given by the implementing acts adopted in accordance with Article 8(3).

For parameters for which no such thresholds are determined, the verifier shall use expert judgement as to whether misstatements or non-conformities, individually or when aggregated with other misstatements or non-conformities, justified by their size and nature, are to be considered material.

2. CONTENT OF A VERIFICATION REPORT

The verifier shall prepare a verification report establishing the embedded emissions of the goods and specifying all issues relevant to the work carried out and including, at least, the following information:

(a) identification of the installations where the goods were produced;

(b) contact information of the operator of the installations where the goods were produced;

(c) the applicable reporting period;

(d) name and contact information of the verifier;

(e) accreditation number of the verifier, and name of the accreditation body;

(f) the date of the installations visits, if applicable, or the reasons for not carrying out an installation visit;

(g) quantities of each type of declared goods produced in the reporting period;

(h) quantification of direct emissions of the installation during the reporting period;

(i) a description on how the installation's emissions are attributed to different types of goods;

(j) quantitative information on the goods, emissions and energy flows not associated with those goods;

(k) in case of complex goods:

   (i) quantities of each input material (precursor) used;

   (ii) the specific embedded emissions associated with each of the input materials (precursors) used;

   (iii) if actual emissions are used: the identification of the installations where the input material (precursor) has been produced and the actual emissions from the production of that material;

(l) the verifier's statement confirming that he or she finds with reasonable assurance that the report is free of material misstatements and of material non-conformities regarding the calculation rules of Annex IV;

(m) information on material misstatements found and corrected;

(n) information of material non-conformities with calculation rules set out in Annex IV found and corrected.